# medicine
# *dance*

One woman's journey into

the world of Native American

sweatlodges, drumming meditations

and dance fasts

Winchester, UK
Washington, USA)

First published by O Books, 2007
O Books is an imprint of John Hunt Publishing Ltd.,
The Bothy, Deershot Lodge, Park Lane, Ropley, Hants, SO24 0BE, UK
office1@o-books.net
www.o-books.net

Distribution in:

UK and Europe
Orca Book Services
orders@orcabookservices.co.uk
Tel: 01202 665432 Fax: 01202 666219 Int. code (44)

USA and Canada
NBN
custserv@nbnbooks.com
Tel: 1 800 462 6420 Fax: 1 800 338 4550

Australia and New Zealand
Brumby Books
sales@brumbybooks.com.au
Tel: 61 3 9761 5535 Fax: 61 3 9761 7095

Far East (offices in Singapore, Thailand, Hong Kong, Taiwan)
Pansing Distribution Pte Ltd
kemal@pansing.com
Tel: 65 6319 9939 Fax: 65 6462 5761

South Africa
Alternative Books
altbook@peterhyde.co.za
Tel: 021 447 5300 Fax: 021 447 1430

Text copyright Marsha Scarbrough 2007

Design: Stuart Davies

ISBN-13: 978 1 84694 048 4
ISBN-10: 1 84694 048 6

A CIP catalogue record for this book is available from the British Library.

Printed in the US by Maple Vail

# medicine
## *dance*

One woman's journey into
the world of Native American
sweatlodges, drumming meditations
and dance fasts

## Marsha Scarbrough

BOOKS

Winchester, UK
Washington, USA

For Beautiful Painted Arrow
...and all the dancers

# Acknowledgments

Great Spirit and all the ancestors breathed this story through me. Beautiful Painted Arrow, the drummers, dog soldiers, moon mothers and dancers collaborated to create the experiences I describe here. I bow in gratitude to all these beings.

Catherine Davis dedicated her time and talent to editing the manuscript, discussing the story and encouraging rewrites. She has been my friend, confidant, sounding board, mentor and "good mother" for many rewarding years. Her friendship is one of my most precious treasures. I'm forever grateful for her loving support and assistance with this project and in so many other facets of my life.

Thanks to Margaret Leslie Davis for believing in me as an author and encouraging me along the path to publication, to Peter and Carole D'Addio for allowing me to care for their beautiful home in Mexico while I wrote the first draft, to David Wilk for lending his professional expertise in the quest for a publisher, to Marian Van Eyk McCain for declaring herself captain of my "support team".

Bill Idelson taught me how to tell a story. Jack Grapes taught me how to write from my deep voice. I honor both of these great teachers for graciously sharing their hard-earned wisdom with me.

I must express deepest appreciation to my hero, Tim Ward, who connected with *Medicine Dance* immediately and brought it to the attention of O Books.

Finally, special thanks to John Hunt of O Books for gracefully bringing my words into print.

For all my relations...

MARSHA SCARBROUGH

# Contents

# Foreword

It has been a delight to work with Marsha Scarbrough over the many years as we both lived our studies inside Native American spirituality. In our work after a while we become the sacred dances, the chanting light of sound and of holy vibrational states of land.

Medicine Dance will take you, the reader, into beyond the deeper states of sacred reverence.

I saw in one of our ceremonies Marsha's personal resonance as that of:
- land
- of washing light in the summer rain and
- of the radiance of the landscapes.

I encourage all to read this new book.

With loving blessings and much appreciation,

Joseph Rael (Beautiful Painted Arrow)
Southern Ute/Picuris Pueblo Indian

# Preface

This story is as true as any written story can be.

In the course of my adventures in Native American mind-body healing, I learned that truth is fluid. It's constantly shifting energy that flows through a cycling universe. What's true for me today may not be true for me tomorrow. What's true for me may not be true for you. An idea may be true for someone next week but not be true for them next month. When we try to capture the truth with written words, we freeze it. The universe moves on, so the written truth becomes untrue for some people at times and true for others some of the time.

Everything I write about here actually happened to me. It happened in a spiral right-brain world where languages only have verbs. By writing this true story, I translated it into a left-brain language of nouns and verbs that describes a grid-based world of frozen facts.

As much as possible, I use real names, although I changed some names to protect certain people's privacy. The character of Phoebe Johnson is a composite of two different women. The events I describe occurred over a period of six years. I condensed the time frame to quicken the pace of the story. Of course, it's filtered through my memory and told from my point of view.

I struggled with how to describe the work of Joseph Rael. He is a genuine Native American shaman, although he doesn't want his work described as "traditional" because he adapts the techniques he learned from his ancestors to fit contemporary times and people of other ethnic origins. I dislike the word "shaman" because I feel it has been overused and appropriated by well-meaning people who do not have the lifetime of rigorous training that is the source of Joseph's supernatural talent. Joseph describes himself variously as a mystic, visionary or healer. Sometimes he calls himself a medicine man, a term that some Native Americans feel is politically incorrect because of its misuse in popular entertainment and association with the scurrilous "medicine shows" of the wild American west. The cultivation of personal "medicine" is central to the healer's power and effectiveness. This focus on developing intuition, inner peace and sensitivity to energy is what distinguishes the shaman. To me, "medicine man" is the term that most accurately describes Joseph's complex abilities. I've consciously chosen to use it...politically correct or not.

Some readers may be offended by the idea of a white woman "playing Indian," a criticism leveled at me by my own family. Please trust that I have the deepest respect for the sacred traditions and ancient wisdom of all people. My way of honoring that wisdom is to attempt to experience it as best I can. I also respect your way of honoring other cultures.

Finally, I want to be clear that I am not an anthropologist or academic expert on Native American spirituality. My story contains information I gleaned from various teachers. Anyone who writes about another culture can only be as accurate as the information shared by informants who tell only what they want us to know. The information I share may or may not be accurate or complete. Nonetheless, these ideas have truth for me.

My prayer is that these written words create a mirror that reflects your truth back to you. M.S.

## CHAPTER 1

# BEAUTIFUL PAINTED ARROW

I smell smoke. I look for the telltale plume of a brush fire in the hills above a modest California bungalow. I don't see one. I take a deep breath, gather my courage, step up to the door and knock. The strange pungent smoke I smell is drifting out through the screen door. A man appears and ushers me in. It's hard to tell how old he is, but his dark skin is weathered. He's probably in his fifties or early sixties. He's dressed in a sport shirt and jeans. If you passed him on the street, you wouldn't look twice. You'd think he was just one of the many Latinos who live in Los Angeles. He's actually a Native American medicine man.

He says, "You must be Marsha."

"Yes. You must be Beautiful Painted Arrow."

He says, "Call me Joseph."

"Is something burning?"

"Yes. Sage."

He shows me dried leaves smoldering in an abalone shell. As he fans the smoke over me, he explains that it will purify me and make me sacred. He's soft-spoken and unassuming.

He asks me why I've come to see him.

"My mammogram came up bad. Suspicious shadows. The doctors have been jerking me around for six weeks. They can't figure out what's going on. I'm having an ultra-sound tomorrow."

I stop talking, but he continues to listen. Deep silence fills the space between us. Finally he says, "So what do you think is going on?"

"The spot they're looking at is over my heart."

"Well, let's see if you have a wounded heart."

He asks me to stand, so he can brush my back with an eagle feather fan to clean my aura. He wields the fan with strong, bold strokes. Whooshing gusts of air cause tingling sensations across my shoulders and along my spine. I feel like something has been lifted off my back.

He asks me to lie down on the sofa.

"Tell me what images come into your mind as I work with you."

I worry that I won't see any images at all. Maybe he's a quack who just soaked me for a hundred and fifty bucks, or maybe I'm a spiritually deficient white woman who has no talent for this game.

My fear doesn't last long. He holds his hands over my solar plexus. I close my eyes. The blackness behind my eyelids begins to glow like he turned on a television screen.

"Wow! I see light! Turquoise light…it's moving…into a ball. Now it's changing into…a cube. It's in 3-D…like a laser light show. And it's glowing…blue. Now it's shifted into a pyramid."

"Good." He moves his hands over my chest.

"I see a black panther in the jungle. She's laughing at me."

He moves his hands over my stomach.

"I see some petroglyph-looking people. They're dancing…like they're having a party."

He laughs and says, "That's good. I'm going to move energy through your body. Tell me when it gets to your feet."

He puts one hand at the base of my throat and one hand at the top of my solar plexus. Warmth flows between his hands, but my feet are cold. He moves one hand to my stomach. Warmth flows...but not to my feet. He moves his hands again. Energy flows as far as my knees, but it still doesn't reach my feet.

"You're not quite ready to walk your talk, because there is something lodged in your heart. Do you want me to take it out?"

"Yes."

"I'll suck it out."

Wait a minute. Have I just agreed to let a man I hardly know suck on my breast? Should I object? His intention doesn't seem sexual at all, and I'm fully clothed. I decide it's OK.

He places his lips on the spot over my heart and inhales. The image of an obsidian arrowhead decorated with a soft feather and a tiny piece of turquoise appears in my mind. He pulls away from me and spits into his hand.

I say, "I saw what you took out. It was a little arrowhead. I don't know why I'm saying this, but I feel like my mother put it there."

"Just think of it this way. You are your mother, and your mother is you. So there's no one to blame but yourself."

That statement pierces me like an arrow. I begin to sob. I'm crying for myself and for my mother.

"Is your mother in the spirit world?" I nod.

"Would you like to bring your mother back? We could call her, and you could have her energy work through you to accomplish something you want to do. You could work together. It would give her a chance to help you."

"I'd love that."

"Good...but first let me show you what it's like to have your ancestors' energy work through you. I'll show you some of my ancestors who work through me."

He dims the lights.

"I'll sit in this chair. Squint your eyes and look at my face. You'll see it change into different faces as my ancestors come through me."

So I squint...and sure enough, his face changes as though transformed by shifting shadows or flickering firelight. His face changes into a handsome brave, an elderly chief, a wise healer, an ancient crone, a beautiful young woman. It changes quickly. Each new face is just a flash as though each character is illuminated by a strobe light.

He's taking me into mystical territory. He's showing me his magic. This is the "non-ordinary reality" I've read about. He's for real. My skepticism vanishes. I feel honored that he's let me see this secret world.

"Wow...that's amazing."

He turns up the lights.

"It's just energy. If you want it to come through you, you have to ask your ancestor for help."

"How?"

"When you go home tonight, make your mother's favorite food. Then take the plate out into your backyard. Using your right hand, drop five handfuls of food onto Mother Earth and say "Hay May Way Who"...that's Tiwa for "Mother, I feed you." After you do that, just talk to your mother like you were talking to her on the phone and ask her to help you with some specific task. Sometime within the next two days you'll have a sign from her to show that she's agreed to help you...maybe a dream. After that first task is accomplished, she'll be available to help you anytime." I ask him to write down the words I'm supposed to say, then I thank him and leave.

As I drive away, I wonder, "Where am I going to find persimmons at this time of year... at 10 o'clock at night?" I go to a 24-hour supermarket. There are no persimmons...but there are strawberries. On Mother's Day, she always asked us to make her strawberry shortcake. I buy strawberries, shortcake and whipping cream. I go home, whip cream, make a plate of strawberry shortcake and take it out into the night.

I feel absolutely ridiculous, but I pick up some strawberries and whipped cream in my right hand, drop them on the ground between the herbs in my garden...and say "Hay May Way Who" out loud. I look around to be sure that the neighbors are asleep and no one is watching...and do it four more times. Then I say, "Mommy, I need your help. I want you to come back to this world and work through me." Then I realize I need to come up with a task. Should it be something easy...or something hard? I consider asking her to heal my breast, but I feel like Joseph has already taken care of that. I want to be able to know for sure when this task has been accomplished, so it should be something specific...and I want it to be something I haven't been able to accomplish on my own...something really hard for me...like making writing into a lucrative career. "Mommy, I know you want me to be successful. I need you to help me sell a screenplay...or write a book and get it published...please?" I immediately feel embarrassed because my task seems shallow. Maybe I should have asked her to help me end war in the Middle East. That night, I have no dreams.

I'd heard about Beautiful Painted Arrow from a friend who met him in New Mexico. Joseph Rael (as he's also known) comes from seven generations of Native American healers. He holds a BA from the University of New Mexico and a MA in Political Science from the University of Wisconsin. He's the author of five books. His mother was Southern Ute and his father was from Picuris Pueblo. Native American tradition requires that healers somehow bridge two worlds. Many are gay, bridges between masculine and feminine. Beautiful Painted Arrow is straight, but he's a bridge between two tribes. The other requirement is that the healer has been wounded, either physically, mentally or emotionally. Healers learn to heal by first healing themselves. When Joseph was a boy, he fell off a horse and hit his head. The accident knocked a hole in his skull that never healed completely. Now the hole helps him with clairvoyance and psychic seeing. At eighteen, Joseph was diagnosed with cancer. He cured himself with the help of tribal healers. His name refers to a special arrow carried in the quiver of spiritual warriors. This arrow was painted with designs indicative of supernatural power. The arrow was never to be shot unless the warrior was in a situation so desperate that there was no other alternative. Once the arrow was released from the bow, its flight would shift the conflict into a different reality. When Joseph says his name in his onomatopoeic native language, you hear the sound of the arrow hissing through the air and hitting its target with a vibrating twang.

Joseph does not consider himself a "traditional" Native American healer since he adapts what he learned from his elders to be effective in evolving contemporary society and for people of many cultures. He describes himself as a "visionary" or "mystic." He says he uses Native American techniques simply because "they work."

My ordeal with the mammogram made me desperate enough to try anything. I was caught in a downward spiral of fear when my friend just happened to call with the news that Joseph was in Los Angeles to do private healing sessions. I booked one on the spot. At least, it was something I could do about my health instead of just waiting for doctors to get around to caring about me.

## CHAPTER 2

# BAD MEDICINE

Six weeks earlier, the nurse had called from my doctor's office. "There's a question about your mammogram."

My knuckles went white as I tightened my grip on the receiver.

"What's wrong?"

"There's an area that the radiologist wants to take a closer look at."

The floor fell out from under me. My stomach sank. The nurse's voice had a patronizing "now don't panic" tone. I gulped air and modulated my voice so she wouldn't hear how much I wanted to panic.

"I'll come in this afternoon."

"We can't take you today. We're booked up."

"When can you see me?"

"In two weeks."

I saw cancer cells crowding my breast, spilling into my blood and floating into every part of my body. I wanted to do something to stop them right now. Today! This minute! How could I live in utter terror for two whole weeks?

I watched my mother die of lymph cancer. She had been complaining about stomach pain for a year before that. More than one doctor had treated her for gastritis or gallstones. When she didn't respond to their treatments, they dismissed the pain as psychosomatic. Finally, her dentist told her that the sores in her mouth were typical of cancer patients. Then they gave her a CAT scan. They found lymphoma in the tissue that connects the stomach to the inside wall of the back. By then, it was too late. The cancer quickly spread into her bones.

As far as I'm concerned, the medical establishment's talk about early detection is hypocrisy. How can doctors find suspicious "shadows" on my mammogram and put me on hold for two weeks? Practitioners of healing arts? Quite the opposite. They practice a form of torture designed to create fear.

My mother was 70 when she died. I'm only in my mid-forties. If I do have breast cancer, what have I done to bring this on? I'm in good shape. I eat right. I exercise. I do work too hard at my job. Have the long hours, stress and sleep deprivation compromised my immune system? Both my parents died five years ago, and my 18-year marriage ended just months after that. I haven't been in a romantic relationship that's lasted more than two weeks since. I have two sisters, but we're not close. Except for a few good friends, I don't have much emotional support. I've been through more than my share of tough times, but I'm not unhappy. Sometimes I'm lonely. Does loneliness cause cancer?

During the next two weeks, I think about my mother a lot. The day she found out she was dying, she was in one hospital, and my father was in another a few miles away. My father had undergone a triple heart by-pass, knee replacements, cornea implants and many other surgeries. Our family had spent every major holiday in hospital waiting rooms for ten years. My mother was always the healthy one. She took care of him.

While my mother was in the hospital for diagnostic surgery, my father decided he would get some surgery he needed to repair an arthritic shoulder. It was minor surgery, but his general health was so poor that any surgery was dangerous. My sister had a new baby to care for, so I took a few days off between TV production jobs for hospital duty.

I went to see my father first thing in the morning. He'd had rheumatoid arthritis since childhood and was pretty crippled from it. His hands were gnarled with swollen joints. His wrists and ankles were fused. He tottered when he walked and sometimes leaned on a cane. He'd checked into the hospital the night before. My main mission was to be sure the nurses had given him his cortisone. He'd been taking it for his arthritis for years and was completely addicted. We knew from previous experience that without cortisone before surgery, his heart would stop while he was on the table. He assured me that he'd taken it that morning. Although he was fragile and elderly, he was still a handsome man with thick white hair and a silver mustache. I sat on the bed and held his misshapen hand. He said, "I've been thinking lately that I'd like my ashes to be buried with Aunt Anne."

I was dumbfounded. My parents had decided they wanted their ashes scattered over the Mojave Desert where they had lived when they were courting. I wasn't even sure who Aunt Anne was or how she was related to us. She had died when my father was a teenager during the Depression. I didn't know where her grave was, and he wasn't too sure either, but he thought it was somewhere in Riverside. I said, "Daddy, I'll see what I can do, but I don't think it's going to be easy to get permission to dig up somebody's grave...and you've already paid the Neptune Society." He sank back into a white mountain of pillows with a big sigh, "I knew it would be too much to ask."

They wheeled him off to surgery. I waited for a couple of

anxious hours, then his doctor came out and told me that he'd come through it just fine. He was in recovery and out of danger. I drove over to the other hospital to report the good news to my mother. When I got to my mother's room, she was sitting up in bed looking pale and sickly. Her eyes were teary. She clutched a soggy tissue in her hand. I told her Daddy had come through his surgery fine. She began to sob.

"My doctor says I'm terminal."

"What?"

"I'm going to die."

"Oh, Mommy…" A few tears slid out before I could get control, "What do you mean? What else did he say?"

"That's all he said." She dabbed at her tears and then twisted the tissue with both hands. I had suspected, from what the doctors said, that she had no hope of recovery, but this was the first time we had faced that truth directly.

She passed the tissue from hand to hand then stopped and looked me straight in the eye, "When I'm gone, you might as well throw away all my origami." I'd told her that the Japanese believe that if you make a thousand cranes, you can cure any illness. During her year of stomach pains, she'd made a couple hundred. Now she was weeping. I had to do something. I went to talk to the doctor myself.

I marched to the nurses' station and demanded to see the doctor. It took a while for the nurse to find him. His "may I help you" sounded insincere. I introduced myself.

"Did you tell my mother she was terminal?"

"Yes."

"Can you give me some more information?"

"What would you like to know?"

"How long does she have?"

"We don't make predictions."

"What? You just say 'You're terminal' and walk away?"

Now tears brimmed up in my eyes. My voice broke. The tears spilled over my cheeks.

"I can't talk to you now. You're emotional." He turned on his heel and started to walk away. My tears froze and turned to burning rage. I leaped in front of him. In a voice as hard as stone I said, "You bet I'm emotional. Wouldn't you be if you found out your mother was about to die? Now do your job and answer my questions." I had him nailed to the wall. I laid out my questions like a Las Vegas dealer. "How long does she have? What can we do to help her? Does she need to stay in the hospital?" He told me she had three to six months. He suggested a convalescent home.

Just as I got back to my mother's bedside, her phone rang. It was my sister. She'd had a call from the other hospital. Our father's heart had started beating irregularly and he'd been moved to ICU in critical condition. I told my mother I'd talked to her doctor and would tell her about it later. I rushed back to my father. He was unconscious, hooked up to a wall of beeping machines. I sat by his bed and listened to his slow raspy breathing until his heartbeat stabilized, and once again, the doctor told me he was out of danger. I knew I should feel relieved, but I just felt numb. I still had to go back to my mother with the news that my father was going to make it, but she had no more than six months to live. I don't know how my own heart managed to survive that day.

After that, my mother hated doctors more than ever. She refused to die in their hospital. After one weekend in a convalescent home from hell, she told me to call an ambulance to take her home. The nurse said, "She can't go. The doctor hasn't given his permission." I said, "You don't understand. She's leaving." She lasted a year and finally died at home. To punish us for our defiance, the doctor refused to sign the death certificate. It took ten phone calls, but I found another doctor who agreed to sign it.

I know exactly what death by cancer looks like. I fought death for my mother and father. I lost the battle both times. I'm exhausted from all I've seen and been through. I pray I don't have breast cancer, but I know I need some kind of healing whether I have it or not.

My friend Christy offers to go to the follow-up mammogram with me. I'm grateful for her company. Her calm presence feels reassuring. We sit in the pale green waiting room reading celebrity gossip magazines. I feel like the grim reaper is looking over my shoulder while we make conversation about movie star marriages in trouble. Christy stays in the waiting room when the technicians call me in.

"Take off your blouse and your bra." I feel vulnerable and exposed. It's cold, and the paper robe they give me is a joke. It doesn't really cover me or keep me warm. The technicians don't introduce themselves or explain the procedure. I don't really need an explanation since I went through this three weeks ago, but a little human feeling would be nice. One of the technicians is short and round with ample breasts spilling out of her open lab coat. The other is a brittle middle-aged blonde who's so skinny that she seems to have no breasts at all. The blonde handles my breast like it's an object that isn't part of me. She lifts and examines and rolls it between her fingers. She lays my fragile flesh on a cold piece of clear plastic, puts another piece of plastic on top of it, then squeezes the pieces of plastic together with a vise and asks "Can you take more pressure?" The spot they are magnifying...on the outside of the left breast...is a place where I had a cyst that became inflamed and then disappeared a few years ago. I remind everybody about the cyst. They don't seem interested. When my breast is flat as a hamburger patty, the round technician covers the rest of me with a lead apron and shoots X-rays through my painfully squashed flesh. It's humiliating, and it can't possibly be healthy for my breast. After that, they squeeze my breast from the sides and do it again. I grit my teeth. They finally release the vise. I'm grateful that this time they don't have to do the other breast. When they're finished, I feel like I've just rolled off an assembly line. I don't know the people who've been handling my body, and they don't seem to care about how I'm feeling. No one offers any information, so I ask, "When will I know the results?"

"Someone will call you in a couple of days."

I feel disconnected from my own body, disconnected from my future.

Christy goes to pick up her kids from school. I go home alone. I'm not sure what healing is or even how to define it, but I know what I've just been through definitely isn't it.

I want to talk about what I'm feeling, so I call my friend Phoebe who lives in Albuquerque. She's not home. She doesn't have an answering machine.

Three days later, a nurse calls. "We have the results of your mammogram."

"What are they?"

"They're inconclusive. We've made you an appointment with a

specialist."

"Fine. Who and when?"

"I made an appointment for you with Dr Snow. Come by here first and pick up the film."

"OK. When?"

"In two weeks."

"You must be kidding! Can't you get me anything sooner?"

"Sorry. He's a specialist. We were lucky to get you in."

# CHAPTER 3

# DEATH…UP CLOSE
# AND PERSONAL

During the next two weeks, I had even more time to think about my parents' deaths. We were one of the "happy" families. At least, we weren't obviously dysfunctional. My parents were not alcoholics, drug addicts or gamblers. They didn't smoke or drink or beat us. They never argued. Never! I'd always thought that was a good thing. As they were dying, I saw that it was the problem. All the anger and resentment that had been stuffed during forty-eight years of marriage was brought to the surface by the stress of confronting their mortality.

My father had been sickly since childhood. My mother wasn't all that healthy herself. When she was a child, she spent a year in the hospital with tuberculosis that had settled in her spine, yet she played the role of his caretaker. Ruby was the strong one, the power in the family. Friends found her vivacious and intelligent. She laughed easily despite being self-conscious about her imperfect teeth. Although she didn't consider herself attractive, she was always smartly-dressed and neatly-groomed with thick wavy hair combed into a striking pompadour. Floyd was quiet, gentle and passive-aggressive. Although they never fought with each other, she would quote the old joke, "When I married him, I thought he was the strong silent type. Then I found out he didn't have anything to say." He thwarted her attempts to control him by hiding behind a newspaper or getting lost in TV. The truth was that their neuroses fitted together pretty well, but when she got sick, it threw off the balance. She needed a caretaker. He wasn't willing to be one. The last year of their marriage became a competition to see who would die first.

My mother's hatred of hospitals dated to her childhood. In the year she battled tuberculosis, she was not allowed to see her family...which was the policy in those days. She was bullied by nurses. She had an aversion to tomatoes that went back to the time a nurse had forced her to eat some stewed tomatoes that gave her food poisoning. During her recent hospital stays, she became agitated at the sight of elderly people kept alive on respirators and force fed through nasal tubes. She researched how to keep herself off life-support systems and had a lawyer draw up a living will. Her doctor had a copy. I had a copy. She always carried a copy with her whenever she had to go to the hospital.

My father did none of that. He took no interest in her research. He avoided making a decision when the lawyer asked if he wanted a living will too. When I asked him directly if he wanted me to give him CPR if he had a heart attack, he said, "It's up to you."

After her lymphoma metastasized to bone cancer, my mother became bed-ridden. Her pelvis had become so soft, it was impossible for her to stand or walk. She had to be lifted onto the commode which caused her much anxiety, humiliation and pain. One day, I arrived just as the nurse we'd hired was putting her back in bed after an unsuccessful attempt to go to the bathroom. She asked me a question that caught me completely off guard.

"Marsha, when am I going to be able to walk again?" She spoke with the innocence of a child. I searched her eyes for doubt or irony or sarcasm. There was none. I wondered if she wanted me to lie to her, but telling her less than the truth seemed patronizing in light of the courage she'd shown so far. I chose my words carefully.

"I thought the doctor said you wouldn't be able to walk again."

"Why not?"

"The bones in your hips have kind of turned into jelly because of the cancer. There's nothing they can do about it."

"I think you misunderstood."

"Maybe I did."

"I want to talk to him myself." She either had crazy courage or crazy optimism. Whatever was going on, she wasn't going to let herself stay in denial.

"I'll get the oncologist on the phone." I took my time finding the number and dialing to give her a chance to change her mind. She didn't. My heart ached as I listened to the phone ring. Once, twice, three times…what should I say if I get voice mail? A nurse answered. I asked if the doctor was there. He was. I said, "His patient Ruby Scarbrough has a question for him." He took the call. I handed the receiver to my mother. She went straight to the point.

"When am I going to be able to walk again?" That's all she said. I couldn't hear the doctor's answer. I just sat there and watched her brow knit, her eyes close, her cheeks droop, her lips press together, turn down and then start to quiver. Tears spilled. She sobbed. Her hand shook as she gave the receiver back to me. I put the mouthpiece to my lips, whispered "Thank you, doctor" and hung up. She curled up in a fetal position and wept. I sat by her bed and tried not to cry. I wasn't successful. There was absolutely nothing to say, so I didn't say anything. I wondered if I had handled it the right way. Nothing made sense. I offered her a tranquilizer. She took it and went to sleep.

She had more than one doctor. The one who was such a jerk when he told her she was terminal was her surgeon. Her oncologist turned out to be a much more compassionate guy despite the fact that golf was always his first priority. He prescribed tranquilizers because "her anxiety is making her excited." No shit! It seemed to me that she was entitled to her anxiety, but in the end, it all got overwhelming for her, and I was glad she had the tranquilizers. He also offered to give her a prescription for liquid morphine when he found out she wanted to die at home. He said the main thing they do for terminal patients in the hospital is help control the pain, and we could do that at home with liquid morphine. When I filled the prescription, I had to sign all kinds of papers. I think they may have even fingerprinted me. She only took it once. When she did, it made her dream that she was tiny like Alice through the looking glass. While she was small, she wandered around a pot of red flowers blooming by her bed and looked up at the huge blossoms in wonder. I thought it sounded trippy. She hated it. She didn't like being out of her body. It made her feel out of control. After that, she never took anything stronger than extra-strength Tylenol and mild tranquilizers.

The night before she died, I fed her persimmons, her favorite fruit. She used to let them ripen until they were nothing but sweet slime and then mix the pulp with cream. Now my mother had stopped eating. My neighbor had given me a bag of persimmons from her tree. I let them get so ripe they were squishy and took them to my mother to tempt her. It worked.

I arrived around dinnertime. She looked shrunken and shriveled propped up against a bank of pillows. Her once-dramatic head of hair was now limp and grey.

"I brought you persimmons."

"Where did you get them?"

"From my neighbor's tree. Here, taste."

She was so weak, it was an effort for her to lift her head up enough for me to feed her. I put the spoon to her lips and let the slippery sweetness slide into her mouth. She smiled and sighed and relaxed back into her pillows.

"Where did you get them?"

"From my neighbor's tree. More?"

She lifted her head toward me like a baby bird. I fed her another spoonful. She smiled again and sank back into the pillows.

"Where did you get them?"

She only took four or five bites, but I could tell she enjoyed every one of them. It was our last conversation, our last meal together. The comforting taste and our quiet connection seemed to leave her content. She rested quietly after that. I sat with my father until about midnight then went home to my own bed.

She died early the next morning. When I got to their house, my father was sitting in the living room, silent and defeated. I went into the bedroom to see her one last time. There was a body in the bed. It was a gray inert thing. It wasn't her. I didn't touch it or kiss it…not because I was afraid…but because my mother was gone. She had left this odd lumpy object behind. It wasn't scary at all. It seemed natural…like seeing rose petals fall to the ground in the garden. The energy that was my mother still existed somewhere, maybe everywhere, like those spent blossoms scattered by the breeze. As I looked at that thing in the bed, something deep within me understood that life is eternal. It wasn't a thought or an idea or an emotion. It was deep inner knowledge. Later I realized that was my first true spiritual experience.

Hospice workers showed up to help us. The coroner's wagon came, and men rolled in a gurney and took away that left-behind husk. My sister and I called all my mother's friends. Many of them said they had dreamed about her the night before. I guess she traveled around to say goodbye before she left. I felt sad, for sure, but I also felt awe at the mystery of life.

My sister and I were surprised at how well my father handled it. All his anxieties seemed to vanish in the face of cold reality. He seemed accepting. He listened as we made the calls. He helped us plan a memorial service. He was clear that he wanted to continue to live in the house, so we looked for a nurse who could stay with him 24 hours. He appeared to be rational and calm.

About two weeks later, he slipped into dementia. He began getting up in the middle of night, wandering around the house, tripping over furniture and falling down. The nurse tried sleeping in his room so she could intercept him before he injured himself. He screamed at her to get out of my mother's bed because she was smothering Ruby. He became violent and strangely strong for a frail elderly man. She tried to restrain him but couldn't. She called me in a panic. I told her that the hospice workers had given us a prescription for a strong tranquilizer in case of a situation like this. I asked her to go to a neighbor's and call a 24-hour pharmacy while I kept my father calm by talking to him on the phone.

My father wasn't sure who I was. He cried and howled into the phone like a two-year-old having a tantrum. "She isn't gone. That stupid woman can't see her!" Everything I said to try to calm him only made him more furious. He yelled at me that I didn't know what I was talking about and threw the phone down. I listened in helpless horror to the sounds of him banging into something, falling, calling out in pain. Finally, the nurse came back and picked up the phone. I didn't want to call the paramedics because I was afraid that would only make him more fearful...and angry at me. Ultimately, we had to. They came, tied him down with restraints and shot him full of heavy tranquilizers. They had to. From then on, we kept him sedated for his own protection. After that, he rarely recognized me.

About two weeks later, he went into respiratory arrest. The nurse tried to call my sister, but it was her birthday and she was out to dinner. She tried to call me, but I was working in production on a TV sitcom where the phones are cut off whenever the cameras are rolling. She called the paramedics. Since no family members were present at the hospital and he had no living will, the doctors were required to put him on a respirator. By the time I heard about it, the nightmare had come true. My father was in the hospital on a life-support system.

I took the next day off. I notified my father's personal doctor, whom I'd never met. She suggested I meet her at the hospital. My husband, Jack, dutifully agreed to go with me. We went into ICU and saw my father. He was shock white and unconscious. His body jerked with each pulse of the machine that was breathing for him. He didn't even know I was there. The doctor who had admitted him was a straightforward man from India. He explained that now we couldn't pull the plug, but I could request no further medications and no heroic efforts from this point on.

"Given his condition, under these circumstances, he'll probably only last a couple of days even with the machines." I called my sister and explained it to her. We both agreed that I should make the request, and I did. My husband didn't participate in any decision-making. He seemed a little stunned by the gravity of what was happening. I was pretty stunned myself. Then my father's doctor showed up. She was a middle-aged Thai woman. Her compassion was obvious. She really cared about my father.

"Let me work him up," she pleaded. "I know I can bring him back."

"I don't know if that's the best thing for him. What does he have to live for?"

"If he's alive, he'll find something. Give him a chance."

I asked the Indian doctor for his opinion. He said, "We don't know if there's brain damage."

The Thai doctor countered, "Maybe there isn't. Please let me do this."

My heart, my head, my soul, my psyche were being ripped apart. More to relieve my own agony than anything, I said, "Go ahead. See what you can do."

She disappeared into the secret halls of the hospital where visitors weren't allowed. I called my sister and told her about my decision. The minute the words were out of my mouth, I knew it was a mistake. I said so. My sister was as numb as I was. She agreed with the decision. She agreed when I wanted to rescind it.

I hung up. I burst through the swinging doors and ran down those secret halls looking for the Thai doctor. I found her snapping on her latex gloves.

"Stop! I was wrong. Leave him alone."

She didn't argue with me. She just lowered her eyes and stripped off the gloves. I wandered back to the waiting room and sat down next to my husband. We sat in numb silence. The Thai doctor appeared.

"I'm sorry," she said. "You're right." She turned and disappeared behind the closed doors. I liked her. She cared. She was a person. My husband put his arm around me. I put my head on his shoulder. My father had left it up to me. There was no way to ask him what he wanted. My best guess was that he wanted to die. I had to live with my decision.

My father died about four hours later. When I went in to see the body, it was still hooked up to the respirator. A plastic tube was jammed into his mouth. The body and the machine were all just one big thing. I felt numb and emotionally detached. The next morning, my whole chest was sore with a dull pain like a great bruise. I had literal heartache. It lasted for days.

After that I hoped I would never see the inside of another hospital, but now I had to go see this specialist about my mammogram...at a hospital. My appointment was in the late afternoon when Christy had to take her son to soccer practice, so I went alone. It was a hot day, but I felt cold. The doctor was a middle-aged white-bread kind of guy with a strawberry blonde toupee. My x-rays glowed on the examining room wall. I shivered in the flimsy paper gown. He studied the x-rays and felt my breast. He studied the x-rays again. I told him about the cyst. He said he didn't see a cyst. He offered no words of encouragement or concern. He didn't say anything at all. I finally broke the silence.

"So what do you think?"

"I think you should have an ultra-sound." His tone was non-committal. "Make an appointment with the radiology department." That was it. I spent ten minutes with this specialist. It cost me $200, and I got no information at all.

I went to the clerk to make an appointment for the ultra-sound. Guess what? I couldn't get an appointment for two weeks. It was like a bad joke... definitely stranger than fiction. I felt like Bill Murray's character in Groundhog Day, only I was living the same two weeks over and over.

Did they really expect me just to wait...wait...wait...to find out if I'm going to live or die? I wanted to do something...but what? Should I put my affairs in order? Start looking for cancer support groups? I could ask my friends for help, but there's nothing they can do either. I could try to obliterate the next two weeks with alcohol or drugs, but I knew ultimately that would create bigger problems. I did allow myself a couple glasses of wine. I drank alone in my silent house...and I cried. Letting my tears flow freely was the most therapeutic thing I'd done so far.

## CHAPTER 4

# MEDITATION AND MADNESS

While I had two weeks with plenty of time for thinking, my brain replayed scenes from the end of my marriage. As my parents moved closer to death, cracks appeared in their relationship. I noticed that their marriage looked a lot like mine. Although my husband wasn't sickly, he was an artist, and I had willingly supported him for close to eighteen years. He was quiet and gentle and passive-aggressive. He was sensitive and artistic. My parents had always disapproved of the match, but the truth was that our neuroses fitted together pretty well. He wanted to be taken care of, and I was willing to take care of him. The relationship had worked up to that point, but now I saw that we would ultimately end up in the same tangle of unspoken resentments as my parents.

On the way home from their memorial service, Jack said, "I'm glad that's over."

"I know what you mean."

"Now I can have you back. It's been hard doing everything around the house by myself."

"You think I've had it easy?"

"No, but I need you to take care of me."

"Wait a minute. I'm a burned-out emotional wreck. I need someone to take care of me."

From then on, he pouted unless I lavished him with attention.

A friend who was studying Buddhism told me about a ten-day meditation retreat in Joshua Tree. Ten days in the desert... in silence...sounded like just what I needed.

Jack didn't want me to go. Actually, what he said was that he didn't want to go.

"You don't have to go, but I feel like I need to go."

"I don't want you to go because I don't want to be home alone for ten days."

"Jack, I'm going to go. You can do whatever you want."

He decided to come with me. He was unhappy, to put it mildly, when he found out that men and women had to stay in separate dorms.

It was April. The desert was in bloom. Tiny yellow flowers sprinkled the sandy earth like gold dust. Hot pink blossoms burst from thick gray cactus pads. The big quiet of barren wilderness felt healing to me. I went on long walks alone. I treasured the solitude. The dry desert floor soaked up my tears.

Jack kept pulling me out of meditation groups and trying to talk to me. I kept telling him that I wanted to keep the silence. He told me that he thought the other people were strange and that there was LSD in the food because he'd been hallucinating. I told him I thought the meditation was creating heightened awareness. At times, I felt like I was in an altered state, but for me, it was a good thing. The next day, he told me that he'd taken himself to the local urgent care center and had his blood tested for drugs. There were none. They told him he was a little dehydrated and suggested he drink more water. The day after that, he told me that he thought the pacifist Buddhist vegetarians were trying to kill him. He had volunteered to work in the kitchen. One of the other volunteers was looking at him and holding a knife.

"Was he chopping vegetables at the time?"

"Yeah, but I could tell he didn't like me."

"If you don't like it here, you can go home. Take the car. You can come back and get me when it's over."

"Come with me. They're taking over your mind."

"They are not. You've been watching too much *Star Trek*."

"I don't want to leave you here."

"I want to stay here. Go ahead and do what you need to do. Let me do what I need to do."

I walked out into the surreal desert landscape and sat on a rock. I stared into a vivid pink cactus flower. It seemed incandescent. Its yellow stamens quivered under the weight of abundant pollen. A single ant wandered aimlessly around the glowing cup of petals. This manifestation of life seemed miraculous to me.

Jack decided to take the car and go home. I called that night to be sure he got home safely. There was no answer. I checked the messages.

"Mrs Garcia, this is the Ontario police. We have your husband."

I scrambled for a pen to write down the phone number I was supposed to call. I couldn't find one. I had to go to the office, borrow a pen and call back. I got the number. I called it. The person who answered didn't know what I was talking about, had absolutely no information and was completely unwilling to help. I hung up. I lost it. I sat down on the floor by the pay phone and convulsed into hysterical sobs. I couldn't stop crying. It was day six of the ten-day retreat.

One of the Buddhist monks appeared by my side. He was unfazed by my hysteria. He didn't try to talk me out of it or calm me down. He quietly suggested that I make a private appointment with one of the counselors for the next morning. I did. Then I cried myself to sleep.

This was my first experience with extended meditation. We were learning a Thai style of sitting meditation called Vipassana. The technique is simple: just sit still and count your breaths. Believe me, it's easier said than done. Sitting still for hours on end is difficult. My limbs would "fall asleep." Pain wracked my knees and shoulders. Staying awake was a problem too. But the most daunting challenge was my "monkey mind" which insisted on constantly chattering and jumping around from one distracting thought to another. Of course, my lively mental activity would make me lose count of my breaths, and I'd have to start all over from one. There was some comfort in the fact that it wasn't easy for anyone. An experienced monk with good concentration might make it to fifteen or twenty without losing count. So why was I subjecting myself to this frustration? To find peace of mind and develop "insight." In the US, Vipassana is called "Insight Meditation."

The next morning, my Buddhist counselor encouraged me to let my feelings overwhelm me again. Between sobs, I told him the whole story. He listened quietly. He offered no advice as I struggled to sort things out. Finally, I asked him point blank for an opinion.

"Do you think my husband is crazy?"

"Well, right now, at this particular moment…yes."

Bang! I got insight! Boy, did I get insight…into myself, into my husband, into how I needed to change my life. Clearly, my relationship with my husband wasn't healthy for me. I laughed out loud. My counselor asked why I was laughing. I told him my insights. He nodded.

"So why is it funny?"

"Now that I get it, it seems so obvious. It's just absurd that I had to go through all this to figure it out." He laughed too.

"Maybe you didn't want to see it because it changes everything."

"And now I have to do something about it."

Jack showed up the next day claiming that while he was driving home, rednecks in monster trucks started chasing him across the desert. When he realized that he was hallucinating, he went to a police station. The police sent him to an emergency room where he was tested for drugs. When the doctors didn't find any drugs in his system, they put him in an ambulance and sent him to the San Bernardino County mental hospital for 72 hours of observation. He was locked in a room with homeless men and drunks with DTs. There was no toilet, so they all had to pee in a wastebasket. The next morning, he convinced the county psychologist that he was OK, and it had all been a misunderstanding. They let him go. The problem was that he was in San Bernardino and our car was in Ontario. He took a 60-mile cab ride and paid for it with my credit card. When he got back to the car, he headed for the meditation retreat to convince me to take him home. His story turned out to be completely true. Later, I got the bill for the ambulance ride. It was $600.

My Buddhist counselor agreed that I should leave the retreat and take Jack home. He offered to give Jack a big dose of Thorazine, which the Buddhists had on hand for just such emergencies. Apparently, Jack wasn't the first person to freak out from too much meditation. Jack refused to take it. It confirmed his theory that the Buddhists were trying to drug him.

I was spaced out from the trauma, the intense meditation and eating nothing but vegetarian food for eight days. I decided I needed some animal protein to ground me. We stopped at a diner in Blythe. I ordered a turkey sandwich. My senses were heightened. I was slightly nauseated from the smell of old cigarette smoke in the upholstery. The turkey felt like rubber in my mouth. It was all I could do to chew and swallow. We drove home. I called the psychologist we had seen for marriage counseling in years past and made an appointment for the next day.

Among the mail that had accumulated while we were gone was a package. I watched Jack tear open the cardboard box. As he fumbled through snowy Styrofoam popcorn, I saw a glint of silver. He pulled out a huge gleaming hunting knife. He'd mail-ordered it. I asked why.

"For protection."

My blood froze. He was crazy paranoid. I knew I was in real danger, but I was able to stay centered and calm.

"You don't need that. I don't want it around, and I'm going to get rid of it."

He muttered a meek "OK."

I took the knife outside. The sun glinted off the shining blade like a poster for a bad slasher movie. I looked around. I spotted a thick stand of wild bamboo in the vacant lot beside our house. I threw the knife into the middle of it. There was no way to recover the knife without spending a whole day chopping bamboo. Still, I hardly slept that night.

The next day, we went to see the psychologist together. We each told our stories. Jack's story was that I was joining a cult, and he was trying to save me. My story was that he had flipped out because I insisted on doing something for myself. She concluded that Jack had experienced "a little nervous breakdown," whatever the hell that meant. She suggested some medication. He refused to take it. I knew so little about mental illness, I didn't even know what questions to ask. At her suggestion, we scheduled regular weekly sessions. Time was up. She was dismissing us and I still had no idea how serious this was, whether I was in danger or what I should do about it. I asked to have a few minutes with her alone. Jack was reluctant to leave the room, but she eased him out. As soon as she shut the door, I blurted out, "Am I in danger?"

"I don't think so. He doesn't seem violent."

"I found a big knife."

"What did you do with it?"

"I got rid of it."

"You'll be OK. He seems pretty passive."

"So what happened? I don't understand what a nervous break-down is."

"He had a psychotic episode, but he has good recoverability."

"What does that mean?"

"He lapses into mental illness under stress, but he gets over it quickly."

"Is he schizophrenic?"

"No. Definitely not."

"But he's paranoid."

"That's a symptom of his psychosis."

"What should I do?"

"What you're doing."

I tried to make sense of what she said. I couldn't.

One aspect of our relationship that seems strange in retrospect was that the sex was always good. In eighteen years of marriage, he was always able to get it up, and I was always orgasmic. It didn't matter how we were getting along. In fact, anger or stress could arouse us. Our sex life was so functional, it was probably dysfunctional. Even that night, when I knew he was sick, and he must have seen the marriage crumbling, we clung to each other for comfort and found solace in sharing pleasure. In our bed, everything worked.

The psychologist attributed his problem to low self-esteem stemming from the fact that I had supported him financially for eighteen years. She urged him to get a job. He didn't like the idea. It made sense to me. I tried to encourage him by reading the classified ads and circling the ones that might be appropriate. I made suggestions. He made excuses to circumvent them. I got tense. Finally, he snapped at me.

"You know we wouldn't be having these problems if you weren't so materialistic."

"I'm materialistic? If I was materialistic, would I have supported you for eighteen years?"

I saw clearly in that moment that I'd been taking care of him like my mother took care of my father. My father was sick physically. Jack was sick mentally. I was trying to change the relationship. He didn't want things to change. I wanted him to be well. He didn't want to be well.

The therapy sessions became negotiations where he tried to figure out the minimum that he could do and still keep the marriage together. I was hurt and disgusted by his selfishness and lack of gratitude, but I was still struggling to make things work. I felt like if I did everything right, I could fix things. If I just knew what to do, I could fix him. I couldn't heal my father, but maybe I could heal him. The psychologist tried to tell me that I wasn't responsible for him, but I felt like I was. What kind of person leaves her mate when he's sick? What would happen to him without me?

"Look what happened to him with you. You were there for him, and he got sick anyway."

"Is it my fault?" I was sitting on a squishy, too comfy sofa. A box of tissues was within easy reach. She was sitting up in a chair facing me. Behind her was an amateurish abstract painting.

"No. Listen, he's got a congenital predisposition to mental illness. Every time he's under stress, it's going to come out. If you stay with him, he may seem to improve, but every time there's a life crisis, you'll not only have to deal with the life crisis, you'll have to deal with his mental illness."

Her stockings made a hissing sound as she uncrossed her legs. She put one lipstick-red high heel beside the other and aimed those sharp-pointed toes at me. I hated that she always wore high heels. I hated that she had long lacquered nails and perfectly painted lips. I hated her golden Farrah Fawcett hair. I wondered if I could really trust her. Could a woman who put so much importance on looking like a Barbie doll know what she was talking about?

"What will happen to him if I leave?" My stomach tightened into a knot as I imagined him muttering to himself as he pushed a shopping cart down a dingy street...or worse, attempting suicide.

"The stress of your leaving could cause him to go into full psychosis. Without you to take care of him, he might need to be institutionalized. If you divorce him, he'll lose his medical insurance and end up in a county mental hospital. But if you stay with him, you'll spend your life taking care of a sick puppy. The choice is up to you."

It's up to me to ruin his life or mine? There was no right choice. Could a woman who's comfortable in shoes designed to keep her off balance have enough gravity in her to know how making this choice would split my soul? I reached for a tissue. My doctor tucked her slim skirt around her knees and said, "I'm sorry. Our time is up."

After three agonizing months, I made my choice and left him. While he was out doing a handyman job, I wrote him a note assuring him that I loved him but needed space to sort things out. I didn't tell him where I was going or how to reach me. I set a date and time for us to meet in the psychologist's office. I carried my heavy blue Selectric typewriter out to the car and put it in the trunk. I took the answering machine, address book and as many clothes as would fit. I drove off while he was gone. I lived in a rented furnished room for a year. I signed my divorce papers on my 40th birthday.

Now I'm really alone, and I may be the one who is sick.

## CHAPTER 5

# MIRACLE OF THE HUMMINGBIRD

The morning after my private healing with Joseph, I head off to see what ultra-sound will reveal. I watch on the video monitor as Dr Snow slides a cold plastic sensing device over my breast. He presses hard. It stretches and squeezes and gouges my tender flesh. It hurts. After Joseph's gentle treatment, the whole procedure seems abusive.

Dr Snow announces that he sees nothing. NOTHING! No spot. No sign of a cyst. Nothing at all.

"I think they misread the mammogram...maybe they were looking at your nipple."

Two days pass. I worry that I haven't had a sign from my mother. I have a couple of dreams, but they don't seem to be related to my mother or the task I asked her to help me with. In one dream, I'm looking up at a huge monument in the shape of an egg. The egg is pale green and translucent. It's glowing slightly as though lighted from within. As I dream, I feel that this monument is important to me, but I don't know what it means. In the other dream, I see a stork flying along a river, and I know he is following the river down into Mexico. I decide I want to follow him there. My ex-husband flies with me for a while then disappears. I arrive at the destination...which is an ugly, boxy stucco house beside the river. The stork becomes a large paper cutout that falls off the balcony of the house and lands with its feet against the house and its outstretched wings in the water.

The next morning when I'm out in my backyard, I notice that my food offering looks just as it did when I dropped it on the ground two nights before. It's not decomposing at all. No ants or snails have touched it. The whipped cream is a little dry but still fluffy. At that moment, a hummingbird catches my eye. I'd noticed this hummingbird about a week earlier. It comes around every morning when I go out to do my exercises. As it zips past me this morning, I see a flash of red, and I realize that it's a ruby-throated hummingbird. My mother's name was Ruby. Maybe this hummingbird is my sign.

I ask it out loud, "Are you Ruby?"

The little bird zips right toward me, circles my head and hovers in front of my face. I say, "Are you my sign?" The bird flies away.

Now I'm completely confused. I call Joseph. He's pleased to hear about the results of the ultra-sound exam. I tell him about the hummingbird.

"Yeah, that's a sign all right. It's even more powerful when it manifests in your physical life instead of in your dream."

"But I had noticed the hummingbird before I went to you."

"Sometimes ceremony simply confirms something that's already happening."

"You know what else is weird...the food isn't decomposing at all. It's just sitting there practically fresh. No bugs on it or anything."

"Wow! It got caught between two realities. That's alchemy! Now that you've noticed it, it will start to change. By tomorrow, it will be decomposing."

I tell him about the dreams and he says, "An egg and a stork...sounds like you're giving birth to a new self...you're mothering yourself. Following the river is flowing into new emotional territory. And I think hummingbird eggs are green."

The next day, there are slugs on the food. By the day after that, it's gone. Every morning when I go outside to exercise, the hummingbird watches me from a perch on top of a wind chime on my patio.

On the weekend, I throw a party to celebrate my forty-fifth birthday. The hummingbird comes to the party. She sits on the wind chime most of the afternoon...flying away only when the crowd is really raucous. Christy is especially fascinated with the bird, because she made the wind chime for me out of driftwood and shells. Finally she says, "Hey, that hummingbird is sitting on a nest." We all crowd around to look...and sure enough, a little circle of mud has been built up on top of the driftwood. It's exactly the same color as the stick, and it's exactly where the hummingbird had been perching. We all worry that we'll scare her away...or that the egg will get too cold while she's away from the nest. But the next morning, she's back on the nest. She adds more mud daily, and the nest gets taller and more substantial during the next couple of weeks.

Two weeks later, I go to a women's workshop with Brooke Medicine Eagle, a Native American medicine woman that Joseph recommended. The topic of the day is "Finding the Wise Woman Within". Brooke Medicine Eagle tells us about ways to connect with our ancient dreaming wisdom. At the end of the day, she guides us on a "journey" to find our wise woman. She explains that the journey is a Native American technique where you trance to the beat of the drum with a specific intention in mind. You travel to the underworld looking for a guide. When you find your guide, you ask a specific question. The guide is supposed to give you a clear answer. It sounds far-fetched. My fear and doubt kick in again. How can just listening to a drum put me in a trance? How can I find a guide? I don't even know what I'm looking for.

Again my fear is short-lived. As soon as the drumbeat starts, my journey unfolds like the images of a vivid dream. I travel through the underworld until I find myself in a great desert. My little hummingbird comes and flies around my head. Then I come to a huge arched rock. When I walk under the arch, I see a giant hummingbird. I walk up to her and give her a bouquet of wildflowers. She takes a little crystal and puts it in my heart in the space where Beautiful Painted Arrow had removed the arrowhead. The crystal is a generator. Its energy is the warm glow of compassion. I know this gift will protect me. The hummingbird has me turn my back to her. Then she stretches out her wings, folds them over me and draws me up against her body. She holds me there until I begin to cry softly. Then she absorbs me into her...or she melts into me...anyway, we merge into one. She's my mother...and now we truly are one. I ask her if she has any advice for me, and she shows me that a hummingbird can fly forward, then hover and decide where to go next...left, right, up, down or even backwards. She says, "The trouble with you is that you think you have to decide where you want to go and then fly in a straight line until you get there. You need to learn that it's OK to just fly...just take off without knowing where you're going. Change directions if you need to. Hover in midair and wait if you need to, but be ready to dart in and grab opportunities wherever you see them. Just fly and follow your instincts." I thank her and ask her if there is anything else she wants to tell me. She says, "Yes. You've been alone long enough now. I give you permission to be with a man again. And you don't have to be with just one man. You can experiment. Go ahead and flit from one to the other...like flowers." Then, as one, we both fly through the arched rock and over the great desert and back to my life.

A few days later, the hummingbird abandons the nest on my patio. I look in the nest. There is one tiny green egg that never hatched. I go through a day of mental anguish.

"The bird abandoned the nest. The egg isn't hatched. The task isn't accomplished. My mother is abandoning me again!"

Then I remember the journey and realize that now the bird is part of me, and I don't need the real bird any more. I decide that the perfect pale green egg in its tiny nest is her gift to me. She's given me a work of art to remember her by, a symbol of sacred potential that will be realized in time.

Not long after that I see an exhibit of wild bird eggs at the Natural History Museum. According to the naturalists, all hummingbird eggs are white.

# CHAPTER 6

# THE PACT

Phoebe Johnson and I have been best friends since we were undergraduates at University of Southern California in the mid-1960s. I was the first person in my family to go to college. I imagined it would be paradise...or at least an intellectually stimulating community. It was far from either of those fantasies.

I was an economically-challenged scholarship student from a "mixed" working class neighborhood. Most of the other students were spoiled lily-white children of the power elite. My fellow students' main interests seemed to be buying term papers, cheating on tests, getting drunk and flying the confederate flag over their fraternity house (in South Central Los Angeles which had been the site of race riots the year before). I missed my home neighborhood where Latino families, low riders and *vatos* mixed with artists, elderly eccentrics and a few leftist bohemians. My mother fumed that my friends were "guttersnipes and beatniks." They were all passionately involved in life. Everyone had ideas and opinions. On campus, I felt disconnected and lonely.

One day I walked by a dormitory door decorated with some hand-written poetry on a piece of construction paper. I stopped and read the poem. I knocked, and a wholesome-looking girl with sandy blonde hair answered the door.

"I like that poem. Did you write it?"

"No. It's by a folk singer named Bob Dylan. Want to hear his new album?"

"Sure."

Phoebe was from Hawaii. Although her father was a successful real estate developer, she also grew up in a "mixed" neighborhood and was homesick for her high school friends.

Besides Dylan, we listened to Joan Baez, Joni Mitchell, Judy Collins, Buffy St. Marie, The Beatles and, of course, The Rolling Stones. I decorated my room with a huge photo poster of Mick Jagger, my heart-throb. Phoebe wanted to try smoking marijuana. I scored a couple of joints from a *cholo* friend when I went home one weekend. We locked the dorm room door and fired up the weed. We turned up the music, laughed until our sides hurt, ate an entire German chocolate cake and a huge bag of potato chips in about half an hour. We started smoking pot regularly.

Since we had no interest in fraternity/sorority social life, our idea of a big Saturday night was to get stoned and eat peanut butter and jelly sandwiches on whole wheat bread. Then we'd wash our hair while sucking on Hall's Mentholyptus cough drops. Under the influence of the smoke, the sound of water rushing around our ears, the sensation of our own fingers massaging our scalp and the intense menthol rush became a near-religious experience.

I coveted Phoebe's hair. She had long straight blonde hair like The Beatles' girlfriends. Our Saturday night ritual often included unsuccessful experiments in straightening out my curls. Blow drying made my hair frizz out like the Afro from hell. We read that Marianne Faithful ironed her hair to take the curl out. We tried that, but my hair wouldn't even lie down on the ironing board. Someone told me to set it on the biggest rollers I could find, so we set it on empty beer cans. It made it straighter, but it also made it stick straight out. It looked ridiculous. I finally decided to cut it really short...like Twiggy...but no hairstyle could make my round, cherubic face look like a gaunt waif. Phoebe just had to comb out her wet hair, and it would dry like flaxen silk. With her green eyes and pale lashes, she could have been a model for Mod fashion, but she insisted on wearing nothing but Hawaiian muumuus and flip flops. It was a fierce statement of her identity. She'd make me laugh by telling stories about the characters in her neighborhood on Oahu's north shore. She'd act out the dialogue in nearly unintelligible pidgin. One story involved a being invited to a family dinner where everyone sat around a big bowl of poi on the floor of a thatched-roof shack. Just as the guests were about to plunge their fingers into the feast, the family cat fell through the roof and landed...howling with indignity...in the tub of sticky goo. In another tale, she convinced me that she and her sister had been stalked by an apparition of the volcano goddess Pele when their parents left them home alone one rainy tropical night.

During the voting rights march from Selma to Montgomery, Phoebe and I, plus maybe a dozen others, gathered at the statue of "Tommy Trojan" during lunch hour. We held placards and chanted "One Man, One Vote." A crowd gathered around us. We were heartened by the show of support...until fraternity boys in cashmere sweaters began to scream "Nigger Lovers!" over our chanting. We ignored them. They baited us. I tensed expecting a physical attack. It didn't happen. The fraternity boys got bored and went off to class. Phoebe branded them "assholes". I agreed with her. The times they were a changin', but not at USC. Phoebe and I were bound together by our righteous anger. We were right. Those other people were wrong. I loved her outrage at injustice.

Phoebe struggled to keep her grades up. I had to keep my grades up or I'd lose my scholarship and my only shot at getting a college education. She was majoring in science because she wanted to be a dental hygienist. She wasn't good at memorizing complicated Latin names, so biology, physiology and anatomy were tough for her. If she did badly on a test, she'd spend far more energy raging at the teacher and trying to transfer out of the class then she'd spend on studying for the next test. The only class we had together was geology, which I elected for my science requirement. She was a whiz with the Hawaiian names for various types of lava formations, but she was lost when it came to the rest of the earth. I helped her study, and she passed geology. She was on her own for physiology, and she flunked it. Rather than face having to repeat it, she dropped out and went to Europe.

I moved in with Jack Garcia, a Chicano artist who had been dating my roommate. She dumped him for a fraternity boy, and he started showing an interest in me. The interest was mutual. He was small, dark and handsome...with thick raven-black hair, caramel-colored skin and a hard muscular body. The sex was hot.

USC began to loosen up. The fraternity boys discovered The Doors. They didn't change their politics, but they stopped taunting hippies and took to singing along with "Light My Fire" at the top of their drunken lungs. By the time I graduated, they were wearing love beads over their cashmere sweaters.

Jack and I got married shortly after graduation, mainly because I wanted to go to Europe. He couldn't afford to go with me unless he could get on a student charter flight as a member of my "immediate family." I wanted him to go, and I was flattered that he wanted to marry me.

We met up with Phoebe in Florence. She'd been living there for a few months studying Renaissance art. She complained that the pasta was making her fat, the bread was tasteless and Italian men were constantly trying to pinch her ass. After a couple days of hitting the major tourist attractions, Jack was felled by 24-hour flu and needed to spend a day in bed. Phoebe and I took a bus to a picturesque village in the hills above Florence. We wanted to hike in peace and commune with the natural beauty of Tuscany, but the Italian men wouldn't allow it. Two young guys on a motorbike followed us as we strolled through the trees…catcalling and propositioning us in Italian the whole time. We retreated into a little café. The men at the bar invited themselves to our table and proceeded to try to paw us. We escaped and jumped on the next bus back to Florence. One of the men from the bar followed us onto the bus, got off at our stop, chased us down the street, into my hotel and up the stairs…yelling "Bella" at us the whole time. We ducked into my room and locked the door. The man pounded on the door declaring his desire in Italian…until Jack got out of bed, opened the door and profanely told him to stay away from his women. The Italian shrugged and strolled away. I burst into laughter. Jack looked bewildered and said, "What was that about?" Phoebe screamed, "See! I told you they were assholes!"

That night, Jack started feeling better, so we all went to a bar to get something to eat. There was a jukebox with the latest Rolling Stones songs. I deposited some *lire* to hear Mick Jagger sing "Jumping Jack Flash". Phoebe was still scared and fuming. I tried to soothe her by getting her to sing along with me …"It's all right now. In fact, it's a gas!" For the rest of the trip, those lyrics were our anthem.

Jack and I returned to Los Angeles, and Phoebe went back to Hawaii. She worked as a cocktail waitress on the Kona coast where she met a young astronomer who liked pot and rock 'n roll. They got married, and he got a job at an observatory near Tucson. We kept in touch. Eventually, she got a teaching credential from the University of Arizona. We've had a few differences, but over the years, our lives have been so similar it's almost uncanny. When her relationship with the astronomer went on the rocks, she came and lived with us for a while. Another time, my relationship with Jack became unbearable, so I went and stayed with her in Tucson for a couple of weeks. We both put the relationships back together for a few years, but ultimately, we both divorced. Neither of us had children. As single women, we'd vacation together. I'd go to Arizona, and we'd go camping at Grand Canyon. She'd come to L.A., and we'd drive up the coast to Big Sur.

Whenever we were together, we made a ritual of watching the sunset. We would stop the car, walk to a quiet spot and sit in silence as the sky streaked with color and twilight began. This was a sacred communion for us. We've watched sunsets from the north shore of Oahu, the wild central California coast, the surreal Saguaro desert of Arizona and the sacred slopes of Taos Mountain. I helped Phoebe move to Albuquerque where she got a job as an elementary school teacher. We started our vacations exploring New Mexico.

Phoebe and I each have two sisters who aren't close to us. Her father died, then my mother died. My father died. Phoebe lost her mother to breast cancer shortly before my mammogram came up bad.

When I tell her the results of the ultra-sound on the phone, her relief is palpable.

"Thank God! What would happen to us if we did get some terrible disease like that? We're orphans. We have no husbands or children. Our sisters don't give a damn. All those months I took care of my mother before she died, I kept thinking 'What if it was me? Who would take care of me?'"

The fear she's expressing is my fear too. She's articulating what I didn't allow myself to feel while I was coping with the terrifying reality.

I say, "We have each other. I could take care of you, and you could take care of me."

"Let's make a pact. If anything bad happens, we'll be there for each other."

"I swear."

"I swear too."

That simple agreement gives me tremendous comfort. The truth is I feel desperately alone.

## CHAPTER 7

# PRAYERS, SWEAT AND TEARS

"There's a sweatlodge Saturday. You should come." Ever since the miracle of the ultra-sound and the hummingbird, I accept any invitation from Joseph without question. I feel honored to be invited. I want to learn all I can about this "magic". When I was a child, my father would take us to the Southwest Museum. We entered through a tunnel lined with dioramas of "Indian life". I was little, and the dioramas were just about at my eye level. I would linger at each one and put myself among the awkward clay figures of women with papooses tending red tin foil fires. I would glide in a birchbark canoe over a mirror lake. I was frightened for bare-chested men with flowing black hair who fought off miniature grizzly bears with tiny bows and arrows. The tunnel was dimly lit and scary. Passing through it felt like an initiation into some great mystery. I was always a little afraid and that was what made the outing an adventure. At the end of the hallway, we waited in front of a big metal door. My father would ring the buzzer beside it. My sister and I would both hold his hand. We'd hear ominous creaking and knocking...then a big final CLUNK! The door squealed as it slid open to reveal a pale old man in a gray uniform. We stepped inside the closet-sized room. The door banged shut. The old man threw a polished wood lever, and the elevator began a slow jerky ascent. I leaned against my father's leg as the elevator chugged up. When it slammed to a stop, the doors screeched open, and we were released into a world of fantastical kachinas, intricate baskets, beaded moccasins and brilliant blankets. There was even a real tipi and a stuffed buffalo. My sisters were afraid to go into the "mummy room", but I was brave. I climbed a spiral staircase and walked along a metal catwalk. Each footstep clanged and echoed beneath the vaulted ceiling. Bits of dust danced in shafts of sunlight that poured in through big arched windows. I looked through a glass wall at the dry twisted remains of a prehistoric Native American woman. Her eyes were empty. Her mouth was drawn open. She seemed to be howling in sorrow and loneliness. It was spooky for sure...but somehow holy at the same time.

On a subconscious level, I must have recognized the wisdom in the Native cultures. Now I can see that their "magic" is a sophisticated healing system that goes far beyond mere physical health.

Joseph gives me an address in Echo Park for the sweatlodge. He tells me to bring loose fitting clothes to wear in the lodge, a towel and food to share afterward. I've read and heard about the sweat-lodge, but I've never experienced it. I'm excited and anxious. I know the lodge is going to be hot, intense and uncomfortable. I'm afraid I won't be able to take it, and I'll embarrass myself by wimping out.

I park in front of an old Spanish-style house. I knock on the door clutching my pasta salad, towel and oversized T-shirt. A woman with cascading blonde curls invites me in. Joseph is in the living room...wearing swim trunks. The woman introduces herself and her partner, a middle-aged man with a strawberry blonde beard who's been studying with Joseph for years. Other people arrive: a Buddhist monk, an accountant, a couple preparing for their

;, an older woman, a psychotherapist, a Native American friend of Joseph's. We change into our sweat clothes. Joseph invites us to follow him into the backyard.

About 20 feet from the swimming pool, in the middle of this perfectly manicured Southern California yard, there's a primitive structure shaped like an igloo. A frame of bent branches is covered with blankets and old sleeping bags. Since open fires are forbidden within city limits, Joseph's apprentice has devised a "rock cooker" out of a gas jet and an old metal pool filter. He uses a pitchfork to pull red-hot volcanic rocks out of the contraption. Joseph gives each of us a pinch of tobacco. He tells us to place our intention for whatever we want to heal in the tobacco and then throw it in the fire. I watch Joseph do this. He closes his fist around the tobacco, brings his fist up to his chest and holds it over his heart. He raises his fist to his lips and blows into it four times. Then he throws the tobacco into the fire. I imitate him. When I hold the tobacco over my heart, my intention becomes clear. I want to heal myself. Each time I blow into my hand, I say, "I want to heal my heart" silently to myself. I throw my tobacco into the fire and watch it vanish in the flames. I see that the energy is being transformed, but how or what it's being transformed into is beyond my grasp.

Joseph's apprentice lights a wand of dried sage and fans the smoke over each one of us. Joseph explains that the sweatlodge is the womb of Mother Earth. When we crawl into it on our hands and knees, we are agreeing to be reborn. The hot rocks represent male energy. When they are placed inside the womb, an act of creation takes place. Water is poured on the rocks to create steam. All four elements work together to allow us to disassemble ourselves, dismantle old patterns and reassemble ourselves in a new way.

When we emerge from the lodge, we are literally new people being born into the world.

This idea makes a lot of sense to me. It doesn't sound airy-fairy or "out there" at all. My frustration with talking therapy is that, as much as it's very helpful for identifying my issues, it doesn't offer any tools that I can use to change myself. It does help me understand why I'm screwed up. It doesn't suggest anything that I can do about it. It's clear to me that the sweatlodge could be a practical tool.

Joseph tells us that the sweatlodge is symbolic of the medicine wheel, an icon used by indigenous people throughout the Americas. It's a simple design: a circle with crossed horizontal and vertical lines dividing it into four quadrants. It represents balance and the eternal cycles of life, similar to the yin/yang symbol of Asian cultures. Beyond that, it evokes many metaphors. The four points where the lines intersect the circle represent the cardinal directions, the four seasons, the four elements, four colors, four animal powers and many other levels of meaning. Those four points also represent the four components of a human life: physical body, mental body, emotional body and spiritual body. According to Joseph, the lesson of the wheel is that when we give equal emphasis to mind, body, heart and spirit, the wheel turns, and our life moves forward in a balanced way. When we emphasize any one over the others, our life gets a flat tire and movement stops. If something has gone wrong in our lives, we need to look at how we balance mind, body, heart and spirit.

Joseph points out that the circular-shape of the sweatlodge is the same as the medicine wheel. He explains that it is built with four doors, one at each of the cardinal directions. We enter and exit through the east door. The other three were closed during the construction, but the "grandfathers" of those directions can still enter through those doors. He reminds us that east is the direction for the mind, south for the heart, west for physical reality and north for Spirit and The Great Mystery. He says that once we are in the lodge, the door will be opened four times, once for each direction. We are to stay in the lodge when the door is open. We are to be silent in the lodge, except when we are praying, but we can show our support for another person's prayer by saying "Aho!"

Then Joseph kneels down at the entrance, touches his forehead to the earth and crawls into the sweatlodge. The others follow, alternating men and women. I hang back and watch the more assured and experienced people. Except for the firekeeper (who has the job of carrying in the red-hot rocks), I'm the last one in. It turns out to be blessing because I'm close to the door. It's dark in the sweatlodge…really dark. People are packed in, hunched over, as close to each other as they can get. It's claustrophobic and uncomfortable, and in a few minutes, it will be about a hundred times more claustrophobic and uncomfortable.

As soon as the firekeeper brings in the first rock, the lodge starts to heat up. Joseph sprinkles the glowing orange "rock being" with dried sage and cedar. Fragrant smoke stings my eyes and makes them water. Joseph urges us to pull the smoke toward us to "bless ourselves". As more rocks are added, the inside of the lodge gets hotter than an oven. The smoke makes me cough. After he brings in the ninth rock, the firekeeper steps inside the lodge and pulls down the blanket that serves as a door. Now it's pitch dark. The only thing that's visible at all is the dull glow of the luminous rocks. It gets even hotter. It gets hotter than any sauna I've ever been in. The heat seems to burn up the limited oxygen. I can hardly breathe. Joseph sings a song in Tiwa to welcome the grandfathers into the lodge. It's a wonderful song, rhythmic and emotional, but I can't appreciate it because I feel like I'm going to die.

Joseph pours water on the rocks. A cloud of steam sizzles up and sears my skin. I breathe in and scald my lungs. Sweat pumps out of every pore. I'm drenched. I'm afraid…of the unbearable heat, of the dark, of not being able to breathe, of being trapped, of dying.

"Embrace the heat," Joseph instructs. "Don't try to push it away. Become one with it."

BECOME ONE WITH IT?! Is he crazy? It's killing me! I just want to escape.

"Embrace your fear. Allow yourself to feel it."

It dawns on me that Joseph is not just speaking to me. He's addressing everyone in the lodge. Everyone is afraid. The experience is designed to put you face to face with your fear. The heat is a metaphor for whatever you're afraid of…a vivid, physical metaphor. The intense physicality makes it impossible to respond to Joseph's suggestions on an intellectual level. You can't just say to yourself, "Yeah, I get it. I'm embracing my fear." The heat disengages the mind. The only way to embrace the heat is to let it soak into every cell. The only way to embrace your fear is to sit there in the dark and be scared. No talking is allowed in the lodge, so you can't distract yourself from your fear by chatting. You can only listen to the hissing water and Joseph's whispered words.

Little by little, my panic begins to subside. I'm getting used to the heat. I'm sweating buckets, but it feels like a warm bath. My nose and eyes are running, but that feels like my body is cleaning itself out. I notice that I'm still breathing, so oxygen must be flowing into the lodge from somewhere. Almost against my conscious will, my body starts embracing the heat. It's a sensation something like hunger. My cells seem to realize that they need this healing, so they drink in the heat. My mind still wants to escape, but my body, heart and spirit are beginning to feel at home.

Joseph prays to the ancestors, thanking them for making our lives possible.

"We give thanks for our parents. We acknowledge that we chose to come through them because we knew they would teach us exactly the lessons we need to learn."

The words express an ironic truth that fills me with gratitude I never felt when my parents were alive. I want to cry. The heat dissolves my defenses. My emotion pours out in a torrent that sweeps away all walls of embarrassment or social propriety. By the time the firekeeper opens the door at the end of the first round, I'm crying like a baby.

No one rushes to my rescue. I'm offered no comfort. No effort is made to get me to stop crying. Everyone stays silent and listens to my convulsive sobs as the firekeeper brings in more rocks. Obviously, I'm not the first person who ever cried in a sweatlodge. In fact, crying is honored as a healthy release.

The door closes, and the lodge heats up again. Joseph prays to welcome the grandfathers of the south, the direction of emotion, the direction of love. In this round, he invites each person to offer a prayer out loud. This is even scarier than the heat because I don't know how to pray. My family didn't pray, and they certainly didn't pray out loud. I've whispered "Thank you God" a few times in my life, but the thought of offering a prayer leaves me tongue-tied...especially after listening to Joseph's simple eloquence.

I listen as the others speak in turn. Some pray for healing for family members. Some pray for guidance in their work. Some pray for healing for themselves. Many of the prayers begin with an expression of gratitude for blessings that have been received, then list family members, friends and less fortunate people in need of help and healing and conclude with a request from the person offering the prayer. Instead of "Amen", the phrase "for all my relations" ends each prayer. Some people use the Lakota Sioux equivalent which sounds to me like "Oh Ma Tah Kwee Yasin." It means that you intend your prayer not only for yourself but also for all the beings on the earth who are related to you...including all other "two-leggeds" as well as "four-leggeds," "winged ones," "swimming ones," "plant people," "rock people" and even "creepy crawly ones." Joseph's Native American friend follows this template, but he emphasizes that each action needs to be accomplished "in a good way." That phrase becomes a rhythmic mantra that energizes his prayer.

After about half the people have prayed, Joseph asks the firekeeper to open the door. As the thick steam pours out into the darkness, he says, "And the prayers go out into the universe." Cool air rushes in as the steam pours out. With the door open, there's relief from the heat and the intensity, but it doesn't last long. The firekeeper brings in more rocks. Joseph sprinkles them with sage and cedar. We bless ourselves with the smoke. By now, I'm so wet I can't tell if the smoke is still making my eyes water. The firekeeper closes the door. The lodge heats up immediately. Joseph prays a welcome to the grandfathers of the west, the direction of physical healing. He pours the water. The scalding steam envelopes me...and it's my turn to pray. Since I'm still sobbing, I keep it simple.

"Great Spirit, thank you for my health. I pray to you to bless and protect my parents who are now with you. Please convey my gratitude to them..."

My tears overflow. I choke out the words through my sobs.

"...I pray to you to show me how to heal my heart. Please teach me how to...love. For all my relations."

An "Aho!" rings out in the darkness. Then another...and another. I stop weeping long enough to hear that other people are sobbing too. Apparently my prayer has touched other hearts.

The prayers continue. Steam sizzles. Sweat flows. Tears fall. Finally, the door opens, and the prayers float out into the universe. Once more the lodge cools down. Joseph passes around a gourd of water, and we are all allowed to take a sip.

Again the firekeeper brings in more rocks. The sage and cedar...the smoke...the door closes. By now, the ritual feels familiar. When the lodge heats up, I'm ready for it. I'm almost getting used to it. I wait for the steam like it's an old friend. Joseph welcomes the grandfathers of the north, the direction of Spirit and the Great Mystery.

Whack!!! Icy water splatters across my face like a slap! I gasp and sputter. Splat!!! Thwack!! Cold water splashes on the people around me who let out little cries of shock. Instead of pouring the water on the rocks, Joseph is throwing it on us. We'd embraced the heat. Now he's forcing us to deal with the cold.

Finally, Joseph pours the water on the rocks. Steam clouds the lodge. Joseph recites a poem that's so beautiful it takes my breath

away. I gasp just like I did when the cold water hit me. The poem
is something about being both the weaver and the web, the
dreamer and the dream, the poet and the poem and the breeze that
blows the whispered words away. I struggle to remember it, but
I'm so spent from the heat and the emotion that my mind can't hold
on to it. Once again, I'm reduced to tears.

The door opens. The prayer escapes into the universe. We crawl
out of the lodge, continuing in the clockwise direction in which we
entered. We complete a full circle. I'm dizzy and unsteady on my
feet. I lie down on the cool damp lawn. My curly hair is soaking
wet. My eyes are blurred with tears and sweat. I look up at the sky.
The full moon bathes me in gentle light. A breeze dries the water
on my pale skin. I breathe and feel my heart racing. I wait for it to
slow down. Once it does, I feel like a newborn baby.

The owners of the house invite us to swim in their shimmering
turquoise pool. I jump in…and can't jump out fast enough. It's as
cold as the lodge was hot. Again the shock takes my breath away.
I lie on the deck. I'm completely spent. For the first time in years,
it's quiet inside my head.

When we're back on our feet, we set our food on a big table. We
join hands, and Joseph blesses the food. Then we all devour sweet
slices of juicy watermelon, replenishing apple juice, salads, pizza,
cornbread and my pasta salad. We're too famished and exhausted
to talk. I ask Joseph for a copy of the poem he recited.

"It's not written down. I just made it up. I don't even remember
what I said."

Joseph tells me that what he does is not strictly traditional. He
believes ceremony must be constantly evolving to meet the needs
of constantly evolving society. He cautions me not to "get stuck in

the form." He admits that some other Native Americans don't agree with his approach. He's been reprimanded for sharing his knowledge with white people.

"But you're still doing it."

"White people are the ones who really need the teachings. If we don't share our wisdom with them, the whole planet's going to be destroyed."

He tells me he's going back to New Mexico in the morning.

"I'll miss you."

"Come to New Mexico for the dance."

"What dance?"

"The Drum Dance. Three days of dancing. It would be good for you."

## CHAPTER 8

# MIRROR IN TINSELTOWN

While I'm delving into the world of sweatlodges, drum journeys and supernatural signs, I'm still living my ordinary life as an unsung worker in film and television production. The work pays well, but the hours are brutal. Days are never less than fourteen hours and often as much as eighteen or twenty. I'm on my feet the whole time. When people say, "Oh, your work sounds fun!" my standard response is "The first eight hours are fun. The second eight hours are a bitch." The truth is that there's very little fun. The days are filled with paperwork, phone calls and catching the brunt of sleep-deprived stars' temper tantrums. I may work all day inside a maximum-security prison or all night on skid row. On rare occasions, I get a day in Malibu or on a ranch in Santa Clarita, but that means driving an hour and a half each way…which makes the day three hours longer.

The good thing is that I'm often unemployed for a month or more between jobs which makes it possible to travel…and I love to travel. I've been to Thailand, Nepal, Japan, China, Singapore, Java, Bali and all over Mexico. Now I'm spending my "hiatus time" with Joseph. The combination of studying with a medicine man and working as a show business grunt creates a schizophrenic life. Part of the time, I'm consumed with exploring mysterious spiritual territory within myself, and part of the time, all my energy goes into keeping one actor from finding out that another actor has a bigger dressing room.

Not all actors are monsters. At every level of celebrity and accomplishment, they may be either monsters or truly wonderful human beings. When I begin to study with Joseph, I'm working with one of the truly wonderful human beings: Marsha Mason. She earned four Academy Award nominations on the basis of talent, not glamour. She's smart, savvy and down-to-earth. Now that she's aging, leading roles are fewer and further between, so she's looking to move into directing. I meet her at a Director's Guild meeting where she's recruiting volunteers to help her with a documentary. I volunteer. Although she's obviously been much more successful in her career than I have, we're oddly alike in terms of our age, work ethic, politics and spirituality. We're both a bit unnerved by the fact that we have the same name. It's more strange for me because my father's middle name was Mason. Somehow we seem to be living mirrors for each other. I even feel safe enough to tell her about my work with Joseph. She's interested and supportive.

# CHAPTER 9

# CRY FOR HELP

Phoebe calls. I hear terror in her voice.

She says, "I have cancer."

"What?"

"I'm going in for diagnostic surgery."

"Where's the cancer?"

"Between my heart and my lungs. I couldn't breathe. I thought I had asthma. I went to my doctor. He told me it was a cold and sent me home with Benedryl, the idiot. I knew that wasn't going to help, so I went to this homeopathic guy. He told me to go back and demand a chest X-ray. That's how they found it."

A chill runs through me. My breath catches in my throat. I feel fear jammed between my heart and my lungs.

"When's the surgery?"

"Tomorrow morning."

"Want me to come?"

"Not yet. Let's see what we find out tomorrow. Maybe it isn't necessary."

"Phoebe, you're young and strong. Lots of people recover from cancer. You'll be one of them. It's not the same as it was with our mothers."

"Yeah, but it sure scares you when they say the 'c' word."

"And it's so weird because we just talked about it."

"I know. I wonder if I jinxed myself by bringing it up."

"No way. But maybe you knew something was wrong

subconsciously."

"Think so?"

"Hey, why don't you call Joseph? I know you've been a little skeptical about the shamanic thing, but what have you got to lose?"

I'd fly to Albuquerque in a minute if she'd asked me to, but I'm glad she didn't. I really care about Phoebe, but I feel like I've seen my share of hospital waiting rooms. Also, it's not a convenient time. I've made a commitment to Marsha. We're days away from shooting her documentary. She's depending on me. Our friendship is developing. She told me she was looking for a feature to direct. I told her I'd written one. I'm hoping she'll ask to read it after the shoot.

Actually, those are excuses. I don't want to go because I'm scared. If Phoebe can get cancer, so can I. I want to push away the fear like I wanted to push away the heat in the sweatlodge.

Phoebe calls Joseph. He tells her he's going to work on her from a distance, so she shouldn't be afraid if she feels movement inside her chest. She goes to sleep and wakes up in the middle of the night. Something is moving around inside her chest. She's scared. Then she remembers what Joseph said.

The next night, my phone rings at midnight.

"Is this Marsha Scarbrough?"

"Yes." I don't recognize this woman's voice, but she sounds panicked. I'm groggy.

"I'm sorry to wake you up. My name is Marilyn West. I'm a teacher at the school where Phoebe Johnson works. I'm calling from St Joseph's Hospital."

"What happened?"

"The tumor was partially blocking the vena cava, the main vein between the heart and the lungs. Phoebe came through the surgery all right, but then the area around the incision started to swell. The doctors were worried that she might suffocate or have a stroke from blood backing up into her brain, so they took her back into surgery and put a tube into her lung."

"Oh, my God!"

"The thing is I'm the only one here. The doctors want a family member present to make decisions. I tried to call her sister in Hawaii, but she can't get here for at least four days. Your name was the other one she listed when she was admitted. The doctors have been asking me whether she has a "living will." I hardly know her. I can't make these decisions. Please come."

"Do they think she could die?"

"I guess so. It seems serious."

"I'll get the first flight in the morning."

Needless to say, I don't get much sleep. Phoebe may be dying. For sure, Phoebe is in a desperate situation, and she's alone. I have to go. I need to get out of my obligations here. I need to get a flight. I need to get a ride to the airport. I need to get a ride from the airport to the hospital. A million things that I need to do spin through my head. At the center of that wheel of spinning thoughts is the terrifying reality that my friend Phoebe, the woman who is most like me in the world, may disappear from the face of the earth before I can get to her. At dawn, I start making arrangements. One hesitation gnaws at me. Phoebe didn't ask me to come. She said to wait. It was her friend who begged for my help. I remember that Joseph said that once you start on the spiritual path, uncanny coincidences show you the way. It's certainly an uncanny coincidence that this happened so soon after Phoebe and I made our pact. I want to talk to Joseph about it. I decide to call him. As I dial, I realize that he's there. He's already talked to Phoebe. He's only about 20 miles north of Phoebe's hospital bed. I get him on the phone and tell him this new development. I ask him, "Should I come?"

"Yes. Come."

I call Marsha Mason and apologize for abandoning her. She's understanding and supportive. I offer her the phone number of another volunteer who can replace me. I fly out at noon.

I love taking off. That moment when the plane breaks free of gravity makes me feel buoyant. With the sudden release, I let go of worries and float above them. This time, the lift off cracks my façade of competence and composure. A great wave of sadness sweeps over me. I'm afraid Phoebe will be dead before I can get there. I weep as I float over the great desert. I remember the lesson of the sweatlodge. I need to embrace my fear that Phoebe will die. How?

The first time I ever saw someone dying, Jack and I were traveling around Mexico in his '56 Chevy panel truck. One hot rainy night in Palenque, we went to a little restaurant to get some dinner, a simple place with tables outside covered by a palm-thatched roof. The restaurant also served as a bus station. We walked in and sat at a table. I noticed a woman lying on another table across the patio. She was a native woman with thick black hair and warm brown skin, probably in her mid-thirties. The waitress and a leathery older man in a cowboy hat stood beside her looking at her with great concern, comforting her. A girl with black braids and huge black eyes was crying and holding the woman's hand. Their luggage was sitting on the dirt floor. They were travelers far from home. The woman was gasping for breath. Each time she exhaled, her breath made a crackling staccato sound that I had never heard before, but when I heard it then, I knew it was the death rattle. I looked away. My eyes fell on a painted cupboard that leaned against the kitchen wall. It was weathered bright blue decorated with red and pink painted flowers. On top of the cupboard was a small fish bowl. In it was a fish nearly as long as the diameter of the bowl. The fish was floating belly up. A dying . woman. A sobbing child. The rattling breath. A dead fish in a tiny bowl. I got scared. I felt the steamy night crushing in on me. I was afraid I had somehow stepped across the threshold of life into the house of death. I panicked. I turned to Jack and said, "Let's get out of here." He said, "yeah." We ran out of the restaurant and drove off into the haunted Mexican night. I wanted to deny death. I was afraid that acknowledging it would give it power.

More recently, I traveled in Mexico during Day of the Dead. The Mexicans honor death by building elaborate altars to deceased ancestors. They decorate their loved one's graves with marigolds and candles...then stay up all night in the cemetery communing with the spirits of the dead. Children eat sugar skulls inscribed with their names. "La Muerta," the smiling skeleton in her stylish feathered hat, is celebrated in pottery, papier mache and papel picado. Now I understand that these rituals are one way of embracing the fear of death. "La Muerta" is looking over my shoulder. How can I befriend her?

I decide to pretend that Phoebe is already dead. I tell myself I've lost her. I pray the Navajo prayer: "It is finished in beauty." I let her go. I weep for my loss...quietly so as not to disturb other passengers. I ask Great Spirit why I have to experience such pain when I've been through so much already...and I get an answer. It isn't like I hear some deep voice speak to me from the clouds outside the window, but when I ask the question, an answer pops into my head. It's "You are being offered an opportunity to create a miracle."

When I land in Albuquerque, one of Phoebe's friends meets me. Rosa Gomez is a big-boned, earthy woman. She drives an old Volvo with a baby seat in the back. She's a teacher at Phoebe's school and obviously very concerned about Phoebe. She offers to loan me her car while I'm in town. I take her up on it. I'm surprised by this hospitality because, according to Phoebe, she doesn't have any friends, and all the teachers at her school are assholes. So far I've talked to two of the teachers who are going out of their way to be helpful. I feel like they really care about Phoebe.

When I get to the hospital, the ICU waiting room is filled with people. Rosa introduces me to most of them. They are teachers who have come to see Phoebe...including Marilyn, the one who called me. I find the ICU nurse and introduce myself as a friend of Phoebe's. She rolls her eyes like "not another one." She tells me I can't see Phoebe because she's sleeping. I ask about Phoebe's prognosis. She says Phoebe has improved but her condition is still guarded. I tell her I've flown in from Los Angeles and ask if I can at least see her even if she is asleep. She leads me to a small room jammed with monitoring equipment. There's Phoebe...looking like Sleeping Beauty...except for the big fat plastic tube stuck in the side of her torso. She's pale but pretty and peaceful. I thank the nurse and ask her to call me when Phoebe wakes up.

Back in the waiting room, Rosa assures the other teachers that they can go home now that I've arrived. Most of them have been there since early morning. I thank them for their concern. They give me their phone numbers, ask to be kept informed and offer to help "if there's anything we can do." Rosa needs to go home to her five-year-old daughter who's with a babysitter.

I'm left in charge, but I'm not alone. I share the waiting room with two other families. One is a big Hispanic family with more relatives arriving every ten minutes. Apparently, a teenage son is the victim of a drive-by shooting. There's a hysterical mother in her mid-40s and a passive father. An adult daughter arrives with a couple of toddlers. A grandmother comes with a pre-teen granddaughter and grandson who are siblings of the victim. An adult son arrives with his wife and child. The mother wails. Recriminations fly back and forth. A verbal fight breaks out between the adult son and daughter. Children cry. When they aren't fighting, they're chattering in Spanish as if they are keeping "La Muerta" at bay with incessant noise. The other family is Native American. They sit in silence. I gather from what little is said that one of their elders has suffered a serious stroke. They arrive one or two at a time, elders themselves except for a couple of women in their mid-forties. Men and women all wear stunning silver jewelry. The massive squash blossom necklaces and turquoise-studded silver cuffs seem to be part of their bodies. They're dressed for ceremony because the potential departure of one of their relations is a sacred occasion. They contain their feelings without speaking. They seem to be in meditation. I try to follow their example.

Finally, the nurse tells me Phoebe is awake. When I walk in the room, she's sitting up in bed. She seems to be breathing just fine. She looks puzzled when she sees me.

"Hi. You look pretty good to me."

"Hi. I'm surprised to see you."

"Marilyn called me last night and asked me to come."

"Why?"

"I guess she was feeling like it was too much responsibility for one person. It's OK. I feel better being here. How do you feel?"

"I hurt like hell."

"So what's this bullshit that you don't have any friends? The waiting room was packed with teachers, and the nurses are all pissed off because you've been getting so many calls."

"I guess I have friends I didn't know about."

Her surgeon comes into the room. I introduce myself. He asks Phoebe if she wants me to hear their discussion. She says she does. He tells her about the complication with the swelling and explains the tube. She seems stunned and doesn't say much. He goes on to explain that they have the biopsy results from the tumor tissue. It's lymphoma. He says her lung is wrapped around the tumor like it's grabbing it, so they didn't attempt to remove it. My mother died of lymphoma. I've educated myself in the details of the disease. I know from my research that they're not supposed to remove lymphomas. In fact, they're not supposed to cut into them because it releases the cancer cells into the body. The proper treatment is to try to shrink the tumor with radiation or chemotherapy. I don't say anything, but I know these doctors have screwed up by taking a chunk out of that tumor and are doing their best to put a pretty face on it. I don't say any of this to Phoebe. The doctor says he'll come back the next day to discuss treatment with her. He urges her to rest.

After he leaves, she says, "I have lymph cancer."

"Yeah. That's what my mother had. I know all about it. It's one of the most curable kinds...especially for somebody young and in good shape. And they caught it early because it interfered with your breathing."

"Shit! Why me? Fuck!"

"I don't know, but I know you can beat it. He said you should rest. Want me to talk you through a little guided meditation?"

"Why not?" She leans back into the pillows with irritated resignation. I lower the bed. She closes her eyes. I whisper.

"We fly across the desert and across the ocean to the Big Island. We go to the land you own where it's wet and warm. Lush green plants grow everywhere. Flowers bloom all around us. You lie down on the moist Hawaiian earth. The warmth of the ground seeps into you and begins to heal you. When you breathe in, you smell the fragrance of frangipani and ginger. You breathe in, and the sweet air rushes into your lungs. There's plenty of air. When you breathe in, the mass inside your chest begins to glow. It turns into golden light. It's just a ball of golden light inside your chest. The ball of light begins to float. It floats up, out of your chest, and begins to hover over you. It starts to spin until it turns into a golden disk. The disk becomes a golden shield imprinted with a sun. This shield floats over you and protects you. You are safe sleeping under this shield on your bed of fragrant flowers... breathing in...filling your lungs with sweet air. As you rest comfortably under this shield, you begin to see that you've become a great woman warrior...a powerful, beautiful, courageous warrior who can create miracles. Your weapon is a sword with a blade of glittering crystal and a handle of carved jade. The sword gives you the power to conquer any illness. If anyone or anything tries to stop your breath, all you have to do is pick up your sword, and you will be able to breathe again. If 'La Muerta' reaches out for you, if she tries to suffocate you, all you have to do is raise...or just see...your sword, and she will let go. She knows she's not a match for you and your warrior power. You are safe. You are strong. You are breathing. You are healing yourself."

Phoebe whispers, "Thank you" and drifts off to sleep.

## CHAPTER 10

# ANGER IN THE AIR

The sun sets. I drive to Phoebe's house in the old Volvo, unload my luggage and find a beer in the refrigerator. I feed her cat and nurse the beer. Lymphoma is on my mind. It's another strange coincidence that my mother and Phoebe were both afflicted with the same disease. I know Joseph will say there's some lesson in this for me. I search my brain for ways that Phoebe and my mother are alike. I realize that they both had the same anger at men. They both blamed their husbands for their unhappiness. They hung onto their anger and made it part of them. Phoebe sees a therapist who's made her aware of her anger. She's even done some breathwork recently to try to dislodge it. Maybe her cancer is her anger coalescing and trying to stop her breath. The surgeon said her lung had wrapped around the tumor like it was trying to grab it. Her body is literally holding on to the crystallized rage, unwilling to release it after all this time. Now it's suffocating her.

I fall asleep in Phoebe's guest room. I get up early and go to the hospital. They've already moved her out of ICU to a regular room. When I find her, she's agitated and upset.

"Where were you?"

"I stayed at your house last night."

"I woke up and I was all alone. I didn't know where I was."

"I'm sorry. I thought they'd given you a sleeping pill."

"Don't leave me alone, OK?"

"OK. You must be doing better. They moved you out of ICU."

She doesn't answer. She avoids looking at me. She's angry. I'm not sure if she's angry at me or at her circumstances. Although I know she has plenty to be angry about, I want to make her feel better.

"Joseph lives up in Bernalillo. Maybe he'll come to the hospital."

"Think so?"

"It's worth a try. I can call him and see...if that would be comfortable for you."

"OK. Call him."

I'm a mere apprentice in the healing arts. This situation deserves a maestro. I go to a pay phone in the hall, out of Phoebe's earshot, and call Joseph. He seems to be expecting my call.

"How's she doing?"

"Better. She's out of intensive care."

"Good. We've been praying for her."

"We?"

"I was going into a sweatlodge with a men's group when you called. I told them about her problem. We prayed for her in the lodge. We all lifted her and held her up, so she could feel supported by men. She's angry because she feels that men have let her down."

"Well, it worked. That's about the time she took a turn for the better."

"Good news."

"Yeah, but she's really angry now. I don't know how to handle it. Could you possibly come to the hospital and see her?"

"I'd have to charge for it."

"I'll pay you." He says he'll come later that afternoon. I tell

Phoebe what he said about the men. I can see the hard lines in her face relax as she lets in the idea of men supporting her. Joseph certainly nailed her issue. I don't mention that, like any healing professional, he charges for a hospital visit. It will be easier for me to ask her to reimburse me when she's well.

Phoebe presses the button to call a nurse, but no nurse appears. It makes her even more angry. I go out to the nurse's station to see what's going on. As I'm trying to get a nurse's attention, a petite woman walks up to the counter and asks for Phoebe's room number. I introduce myself. She tells me she's Tillie, an old friend of Phoebe's, who flew in from Tucson as soon as she heard the news. I'm surprised. I thought Phoebe didn't have any close friends in Arizona. When she was debating whether to move to Albuquerque, she asked for my opinion. I said, "Get out! You've done nothing but complain about the people since you moved there. If you go to Albuquerque, you can start over and make new friends." Yet here's a friend who cares enough to buy a ticket, leave her husband and child behind and fly in to offer support without even being asked. I take Tillie to Phoebe's room. Phoebe seems as surprised to see her as I am.

I go eat lunch in the cafeteria so they can talk alone. It actually has pretty good food (even a salad bar and frozen yogurt), but all hospital cafeterias have the same sorrowful clientele...people who are too distressed to eat and staff who don't have time to enjoy a meal. I think about all the holiday meals I've eaten with my family in cafeterias just like this one. Then I wonder why Phoebe is able to attract so many friends when she doesn't seem to appreciate them. I ask myself why I've chosen Phoebe as a friend. We have a lot in common: our politics, our taste in music, our love of nature. These other friends may not even share those interests…but they all want to help. I'm helping Phoebe too…and I've helped her in the past. I helped her pass geology. I gave her a home when she left her husband. I helped her move from Tucson to Albuquerque. I realize that Phoebe's ever-present anger is actually an expression of helplessness. Since most people are essentially decent, they want to help people in need. Indirectly, Phoebe is forever asking for help, but she doesn't recognize the people who offer it as friends. Do I do the same thing? I decide that I'm quite the opposite…and that's why our friendship works. I think I project a competent persona that dovetails with her frustrated victim. It occurs to me that it's the same kind of relationship I had with my husband.

I go back to Phoebe's room and join the conversation. Joseph shows up shortly after that. I introduce him to Phoebe. I suggest that Tillie and I retreat to the waiting room so Joseph and Phoebe can work alone. I think he may want to do some healing work on her like he did on me. While we wait, Tillie tells me that she worked with Phoebe in the geology department office at the University of Arizona, and they stayed friends after they both left their jobs. Phoebe never mentioned the friendship to me although she'd told me volumes about all the people she didn't get along with in the geology department.

Joseph joins us after about twenty minutes. I don't ask him what went on because I know he has to keep that confidential, just like any shrink or priest or lawyer. I do ask him what we can do for her. I tell him Phoebe has a lot of friends who want to help. He suggests a sweatlodge dedicated to her healing. We schedule one for the next night at his place in Bernalillo. I write him a check for $200.

He leaves. We go back to Phoebe's room. I ask how it went.

"Fine. We just talked. I like that he's so quiet and gentle."

That's all she has to say about it.

The sun goes down. Tillie's tired from traveling. Visiting hours are over. I suggest that Tillie take Rosa's car back to Phoebe's house and get some sleep. I'll stay with Phoebe all night as I promised. Tillie can relieve me in the morning. She agrees to the plan. A nurse comes in to prepare Phoebe for bed. She tells me it's time for me to leave. I ask her to step out in the hall with me. I tell her about how Phoebe was frightened when she woke up in the night and that I promised I wouldn't leave her alone. The nurse says it's against the rules, but she'll look the other way. If I don't disturb anyone, she'll let me sit in the chair by Phoebe's bed all night long. So that's what I do. I try to sleep without much luck. Phoebe calls out in the night a few times. When she does, I touch her and assure her that I'm there. The hospital is eerie at night. The darkness is still except for the sounds of labored breathing and occasional moans of pain. The light and bustle of day keeps "La Muerta" in the background, but I feel her sitting right beside me in the shadow world of night. I shift in my chair and try a thousand different positions. None are comfortable. When the sun finally rises, Phoebe wakes up refreshed. I feel like I've been hit by a truck.

As soon as Phoebe finishes breakfast, a doctor she's never seen before marches into the room and announces that he's going to take a bone marrow sample. I know this is one of the most painful procedures in medicine. I know they need it to figure out how far the cancer has progressed and whether Phoebe could be a candidate for a bone marrow transplant. The doctor doesn't explain any of this. I think springing something so painful on Phoebe is a bad idea. It's sure to piss her off midway through and make the whole thing that much more difficult. I decide to speak up.

"Doctor, can you tell us about what you want to do, so we'll know what's going on?" He explains that he'll puncture Phoebe's low back with two large hollow needles then punch them into her pelvic bone and remove some bone marrow to test for cancer cells.

I say, "Phoebe, that's got to be a real bitch. Would it be helpful if I stay in the room with you?"

She says, "Yes." The doctor agrees to it. Two nurses appear to assist him. Phoebe lies face down. They inject a local anesthetic into either side of her back, just below her waist and above her butt. Then they pull out the needles. I'm glad she's lying face down so she can't see them. They are the size of ten-penny nails. They have to be that big to punch through the pelvic bone. Basically, they're going to pound nails into her back. I stroke her hair gently as the doctor leans his weight onto the needle until it makes a sickening crunch when the bone gives way. Phoebe can't see them suck foamy red marrow into glass tubes. I just keep telling her she's doing great and it won't be much longer. When it's finally finished and Phoebe is trying to find a way to sit on her wounded ass, Jerry Springer comes on the hospital TV. I say to the doctor, "I hear your ex-wife is going to be on today to talk about all the ways you tortured her." The doctor, Phoebe and the nurses all laugh out loud. The laughter does more to disperse the pain than any drug. Tillie finally shows up just as they're leaving. I go back to Phoebe's house and fall asleep.

When I wake up, I call all of Phoebe's friends and tell them about the sweatlodge. It's short notice. Some people have other obligations. Some people are put off by the idea. Some people are enthusiastic and promise to be there.

By the time I get back to the hospital, Phoebe's sister Lenore has arrived from Hawaii. She looks pale, shaken and tired. I've barely introduced myself to her, when a nurse comes in and announces that Phoebe is being moved to another room. No one is sure why this move has been ordered. It seems like an unnecessary disruption. I go to find a supervising nurse to see if I can prevent it. I can't find anyone who will admit to having the authority to do anything about it. I go back to Phoebe's room, but she's gone. Lenore stuffs Phoebe's few possessions into an overnight bag. As we walk to Phoebe's new room together, Lenore tells me that she isn't feeling well. She feels like she has stomach flu. I ask if it could be the combination of anxiety, stress and jet lag. She acknowledges that she's suffering from all of those. She seems more emotionally fragile than any of us. I suspect the reason she took so long to get here was that she needed two days to get her courage up. After all, Hawaii is only a five-hour flight away.

When we get to Phoebe's room, we step into chaos. She's upset because she can't find things including her wallet and address book. She's expecting phone calls and is worried that friends don't have her new room number. That morning, the doctor told her that her cancer was "stage two," and none of us knows what that means. He wants her to get in touch with the local Wellness Center and find out about support groups. Friends called and said they sent flowers, but no flowers have been delivered. She's overwhelmed and borderline hysterical. Tillie rummages through everything looking for the missing items. Phoebe feels like her life is spinning out of control. The same thing happened with my mother more than once. I know what to do.

"Listen, there is a lot to be dealt with, but there are three of us. We can divide up the problems and solve them all. Lenore, find out if there's a hospital library where you can go look up what 'stage two' means. They should also have the number of the Wellness Center. Call them and see if they can send someone over with information for Phoebe. Tillie, go see if you can track down the flowers. They may have been sent to the old room. I'll help Phoebe get organized and put things away. I know we'll find the wallet and address book in the process."

Lenore hurries off to find the library. Tillie sits on the end of Phoebe's bed and doesn't say a word. I start going through Phoebe's things systematically. I ask her where she wants each item. On her rolling tray? In the nightstand drawer? In her cupboard? I put every decision in Phoebe's hands. A Candy Striper comes in. Phoebe asks her about the flowers. The girl goes out to check on them. The address book appears. I find Phoebe's wallet in her purse. A nurse brings in a lunch tray. I realize I'm starving. I'm exhausted. I need to take care of myself.

"Tillie, would you like to go out to lunch with me while Phoebe eats?"

She nods. I can't take the hospital cafeteria again. There's a cute bistro across the street called The Artichoke Café. We get a table. The café has exposed brick walls, hardwood floors, white tablecloths and a lemon slice in the water. Convivial conversations bubble at the tables around us. It feels civilized. I begin to relax. Tillie puts down her menu and nails me with her gaze.

"Don't give me orders. You have no right to tell me what to do."

Her anger feels like a slap across my face. Her harshness slices straight through my thin veneer of strength. I'm too depleted to defend myself. I start to weep. She's speechless. She was looking for a fight...and she didn't get one.

"I'm really sorry. I was just trying to help Phoebe. Of course, you're right. I was bossy."

"I want to decide what I'm going to do."

"I'll try not to do it again. If I do, please forgive me. I'm really stressed-out and exhausted."

"But you seem so capable and strong."

"Phoebe needs somebody to lean on."

Tillie was right. I'd been giving orders. I saw chaos, and I wanted to create order. Things were breaking down, and I wanted to fix them. No one seemed to know what to do, so I took charge. I'd been arrogant and overbearing. Maybe I did it to feel powerful. Maybe I did it to get things done.

I order salade Nicoise. I explain to Tillie that my job in film production is to take charge of the crew and solve problems as they come up.

"I guess I was getting my work and my personal life confused. Feel free to call me on it if I do it again." All seems forgiven. Tillie and I bond over lunch.

When we get back to Phoebe's room, flowers are arriving. Lenore returns with a report that "stage two" means that cancer has invaded two quadrants of the body. In other words, it's at an intermediate stage between early and advanced. I suggest that Lenore take the car, stop by the Wellness Center to pick up literature, and then go home to rest before the sweatlodge. Phoebe is still afraid of being alone at night. Tillie volunteers to spend the night at the hospital.

# CHAPTER 11

# WOMEN ALIVE

When it's time to leave for the sweatlodge, Lenore doesn't want to go. She feels sick and thinks she'd be better off in bed. I point out that the sweatlodge is a great way for her to heal herself and Phoebe at the same time. Then she admits that she's scared by the whole idea of the darkness and the heat.

"That's a natural reaction. You don't have to go in if you don't want to, but come and be part of the group intention of healing Phoebe. You can stay outside by the fire and meditate while we're in the lodge."

She agrees to come. As we drive north, the city begins to thin. The bleak majesty of high desert stretches out around us. The vastness seems to open up my head and free it from the confines of narrow florescent-lit hospital hallways. I breathe in the soft twilight as we turn off at Bernalillo. Joseph's place turns out to be a permanently-parked antique mobile home in a suburban neighborhood of pre-fab houses. Neighbors' yards hold swing sets and blue plastic wading pools, but Joseph's narrow strip of land is crammed with a sweatlodge, a fire pit and a round adobe structure that he calls a "kiva." Railroad tracks run three feet outside the back fence of his property. It's hardly the serene natural setting I'd pictured.

We gather in the kiva, which Joseph built the same way that ancient Americans built their sacred structures. It's a cylinder of adobe with a sunken altar in the middle of a packed-dirt floor. The round candle-lit room is warm, comfortable and filled with the rich fragrance of earth. Besides me and Lenore, several teachers show up including Rosa. Phoebe's breathwork therapist is also there. Joseph introduces a woman, Carolyn Powell, who heard about Phoebe's situation from Joseph and wants to participate even though she doesn't know Phoebe personally. I thank her for her support. Aside from Joseph, the group is entirely women. He gives his usual introductory explanation of the sweatlodge ceremony and invites us to follow him into the lodge. Lenore announces that she'll stay outside the lodge. Joseph asks why. She says she's too scared to go in.

Joseph says, "Think about how scared your sister is. She has no choice. If she can stand that, can't you stand to be scared for a couple of hours? Can't you make a sacrifice to help her?"

Lenore says she can. She goes into the lodge. The ceremony is powerful. Joseph says very little. The temperature is scorching, and emotions run even hotter. I beseech Great Spirit to let my friend live. I cry buckets…for Phoebe and for myself. This is the one place where I don't have to be strong. The heat and the fatigue break down all my defenses. Lenore cries too. When it's her turn to pray, all she says is "I love my sister so much. I love my sister so much" over and over.

After the lodge, I take Joseph aside and ask him about Lenore's health.

"She says she feels like she has the flu. I think she just can't take the stress. I feel like I have to take care of her as well as Phoebe."

"She's afraid to feel her own emotions. She's going to be sick for about ten days."

"She's only going to be here ten days."

"I know."

"So I'm going to have to take care of both of them as long as she's here."

"You got it."

That night I dream that I'm in my own living room. I turn on the lights, and my cats scatter. Some other creature that I can't identify runs and hides inside a golf bag resting against my dining room table. I walk over to look at the animal and notice that my cats have vomited on the rug. Then they begin vomiting in front of me and licking it up. As I get close, the animal runs out of the golf bag. It's a cottontail rabbit. I decide to let it live in my house. During this dream, my hands are tingling with energy. I have a sense that the dream is about "handing" healing energy to others.

When I wake up, I tell the dream to Lenore. She says that when she came home from the hospital nauseated, Phoebe's cat vomited a huge quantity in front of her. She finds it unsettling because she had 24-hour stomach flu six times in the past four months.

I tell Joseph about the dream. He says the cats are our familiars. By vomiting they are taking the poison of the cancer out of us and expelling it. The rabbit represents fear and the opening heart. Allowing the rabbit to live in my house means that I'm allowing fear and love to exist simultaneously in my life. He feels the golf clubs come from a Native American myth about a hunter of wisdom. The hunter travels to the upper world and does battle with a sun god who has taken his father's head. The hunter finds the sun god playing shinny (a game like golf) with his father's head. The hunter's ally advises him to carve his own shinny sticks (which are like golf clubs) and use them to break the sun god's shinny sticks.

He takes the advice, defeats the sun god and is able to bring his father's head down to earth. He brings his father back to life by reattaching his father's head...which represents integrating heart and mind. The golf clubs are the tool used to accomplish this wholeness of self. According to Joseph, the energy I felt in my hands when I was dreaming was caused by heart energy rushing into my extremities as my mind and heart integrated. He tells me that 80 percent of the healing Phoebe will experience is because I'm there for her.

Phoebe heals quickly. At least, she heals from the surgery. The cancer will require chemotherapy. Her surgeon and her oncologist agree to allow her to go home and schedule her for chemo as an outpatient. She's happy about being able to leave the hospital, but she's unhappy about the prospect of being sick from chemotherapy. She'd been looking forward to planting a garden in the backyard of the house she bought a couple of months before. When she finds out that chemo means two or three months of nausea and low energy, she hangs her head like a martyr and says, "I guess I won't be able to plant my garden this year." Her victimized resignation hooks the compulsive problem-solver in me.

"You've got lots of friends who want to know what they can do to help. Tell me what you want planted where. I'll see to it that your garden gets planted."

After seven days, Phoebe is released from the hospital. It's Saint Patrick's Day. We stop at Marilyn's house on the way home. It's her birthday, and she invites us to celebrate with her. We eat birthday cake, but what we're really celebrating is the fact that Phoebe is still alive. Phoebe faced death. Marilyn, Tillie, Lenore and I stood beside her. So far, we've faced death down, and we feel pretty powerful. Phoebe is more vivacious than I've ever seen her. She looks at the women who've been there for her with real love in her eyes. We take a group photo with smiles blazing. For about three hours, Phoebe doesn't say a bitter word.

When the party is over, we go to Phoebe's house. All four of us are staying there. Lenore and I each have a twin bed in the guest room. Tillie moves out of Phoebe's bedroom onto the sofa. Phoebe's tired and starts getting ready for bed. I ask her if she'd like to create an altar dedicated to her healing in her bedroom. She replies that it couldn't hurt. I'm pleased that she's taking responsibility for her physical healing, but I feel she also needs to address the psychological, emotional and spiritual causes of her disease. I'm glad she's open to the idea of an altar. While she sleeps, I scour the house for objects to put on the altar. I can't find anything with any spiritual context. I remember that I have a laminated card of the Virgin of Guadalupe and a little plastic figure of Kwan Yin, the feminine Bodhisattva of compassion. I use those as the focus of the altar and surround them with a small vase of fresh flowers, an amethyst crystal, a glass of water and a votive candle. I rest peacefully that night.

While I'm making breakfast in the morning, Tillie takes me aside.

"Phoebe woke up in the night and saw that candle burning in her room. She was very upset that you lit a candle and didn't tell her about it. That's a fire hazard. She asked me to tell you not to do that again."

I feel like I just got my wrists slapped for a minor misunderstanding. When Phoebe comes to breakfast, I say to her directly,

"Sorry about the candle. Next time, I'll wake you up and ask you." She doesn't reply. I feel like she must see me as powerful and is looking for a way to let me know I'm not.

In the afternoon, Tillie flies back to Tucson. I take her to the airport. At the gate, I tell her that she was a great help, "I'm so glad you showed up."

She says, "I learned a lot from you. You are truly love in action." I'm surprised that she's changed her opinion of me so radically. I'm a little embarrassed by the compliment, but I finally manage to say, "I'm deeply flattered because I know you don't hesitate to say what you really feel."

We hug and promise to keep in touch.

Phoebe's chemo starts the next day. We plan one last high-caloric blow-out before the months of nausea. Phoebe's former neighbors, Carlos and Joaquin, propose the plan and offer to prepare the feast. They're a gay couple who put Martha Stewart to shame. When Phoebe, Lenore and I arrive at their beautifully decorated home, they immediately offer us drinks and great greasy cheesy nachos. A centerpiece of fresh flowers graces the table which is graciously set with fine china. They fuss over all of us, give Phoebe special attention, cook up a storm and make amusing conversation...all at the same time. They're warm and friendly and obviously care about Phoebe. Again, I find myself wondering why Phoebe never mentioned them to me. The food is a fiesta of cholesterol. Nachos followed by a chicken casserole with green chili, jack cheese and cream sauce. The finale is a huge tart with a crust of cookie dough spread with cream cheese topped with sliced fresh fruit glazed with apricot jam. Later, Lenore confesses that the desert was so sweet, she went in the bathroom and rinsed out her mouth after she ate it. Of course, Phoebe and I have never had any difficulty consuming sweets. In the afterglow of that gastronomic orgy, I bring up the subject of Phoebe's garden. Carlos and Joaquin immediately offer to come over with their Rototiller and work the soil. Phoebe accepts the offer. We schedule it for Sunday.

The next day, I take Phoebe to the hospital for her first chemotherapy session. Lenore doesn't go with us because she still isn't feeling well. Phoebe and I go to an outpatient office. A nurse invites her to sit in a big recliner-type of chair. The nurse has trouble finding a vein for the IV needles. She urges Phoebe to consider having a catheter inserted through her chest so they can hook her up more easily. She finally connects Phoebe to a bunch of plastic tubes. Phoebe gets pretty mellow because one of the bags of liquid they're dripping into her has a tranquilizer in it. I read the literature they gave her explaining what all the chemicals are. It's scary reading because everything is highly toxic. The idea behind chemo is to pump enough poison into your body to kill the fast-growing cancer cells. The trick is to stop before too much damage is done to everything else. The problem is that the poison that kills cancer cells also kills every other kind of fast-growing cell...like hair, fingernails and mucus membranes. Dead mucus membranes in your digestive tract cause nausea. Dead hair falls out. Fingernails often turn black. Sometimes teeth crumble and fall out.

After about five bags of toxic chemicals are dripped into Phoebe's veins, I drive her home. They've given her state-of-the-art anti-nausea medicine, so she takes some before she goes to bed to sleep off the tranquilizer. I wash the breakfast dishes while she sleeps. I break a glass in the process. I sweep up the shards and throw them in the trash.

A weathered grape-stake fence encloses Phoebe's back garden. Carlos and Joaquin advise us that it needs to be painted with motor oil to keep it from deteriorating in the harsh desert weather. They don't volunteer for that job, but they tell me I can go to any auto parts store and get the cheapest grade of oil. I do, and then I go to the hardware store and get big paint brushes. I stop at a market and get beer, so we'll have some to offer Carlos and Joaquin after their Rototilling efforts.

When I get back, Phoebe and Lenore attack me the moment I walk in the door. In the process of taking out the kitchen trash, Phoebe pushed the contents of the trash can to compress them and narrowly missed cutting her hand on the broken glass I'd tossed in there. Nothing happened. Phoebe was not hurt at all, but Lenore scolds me furiously, then lectures me on the proper procedure. I must put broken glass in a separate bag, seal it with tape, take a marker and label it "Sharp" before discarding it. I tell her I've never heard that in my life, but it sounds like a good idea. She says that's what they always do in the dentist's office where she works. Phoebe is being a drama queen, "What if I'd cut my wrist? I could have gotten an infection. How could you be so careless?" I realize these women need to make me feel stupid. I guess opportunities to criticize me are so rare that they need to get as much mileage out of this one as they can. Intellectually, I understand that putting me down makes them feel powerful, but it still hurts my feelings. Their pettiness makes me angry, but I feel guilty about getting mad at a couple of sick people.

I take my motor oil and go out to paint the fence. I paint with a vengeance. It's the perfect activity for expressing my rage. I slap black ooze on dry splitting wood and watch it disappear into the cracks. Oil splatters my face. My hands get stained. Dirt sticks to my oily fingers. The sun bakes me and the thirsty fence. Sweat pours off me and mixes with the oil and grime. It's good, honest work that leaves me exhausted and dirty.

While I take on the fence, Phoebe naps and Lenore lounges. Lenore comes out to check my work once, then retreats back inside the house. When I finish, the fence doesn't look much different. It's a darker brown and has a slight sheen. It smells like an auto repair shop, and so do I. I take a long hot shower, drink one of the beers and go to sleep.

The next day, the guys show up with the Rototiller. They work like champs. The awkward, insect-looking machine chews through cement-hard desert soil like a hungry monster. I dump bags of fertilizer into the tiller's path. A job that would have been a brutal day's work for me is done in a couple of hours. Phoebe watches in awe. I don't think she realized what a tough job "planting a garden" really is. She would have needed help if she was in perfect health. When they finish, I offer them the beers. We drink and laugh for another hour.

Now Phoebe's garden is ready to be planted. She just needs to come up with a design and figure out what plants to buy. We put plastic chairs on the cultivated earth and sit in the vacant space to contemplate the possibilities. I see the garden as a metaphor for Phoebe's healing. Supportive friends helped her with the dirty work. Now she has to design her life so it can flower. It's time for her to put her attention on what she wants instead of just complaining about what she lacks. That night, Lenore starts to feel better. She flies back to Hawaii the next day.

Phoebe and I take her to the airport. Lenore thanks me for taking care of her sister. She's fragile and weepy. She promises to be better about keeping in touch with Phoebe. I feel like that's a promise she's too vulnerable to keep. Each sister says she loves the other.

On the way home, we stop at K-Mart. Phoebe buys lace curtains for her bedroom. We both pick up a few things to replenish supplies. The effects of the chemo are diminishing, and Phoebe's feeling pretty good. We go to lunch at Garcia's and stuff ourselves with down-home Mexican food. Since Phoebe's doctor has encouraged her to eat whatever she feels like eating during chemo, we stop at the market and lay in a supply of Haagen Dazs.

In the evening, Phoebe wants to take a bath in Epsom salts because it's supposed to relieve the chemo side-effects. She bought Epsom salts at K-Mart, but now she can't find them. She storms around the house slamming cupboard doors and spouting obscenities. She blames the cashier for not putting them in the bag. She curses the "stupid Epsom salts". She pouts about not being able to do what she wants to do. I try to help. I look in all the logical places. I open a drawer under her linen cupboard and find a box of Epsom salts. I take it to her.

She rips the box from my hand and screams in my face.

"Damn you! You never let me have my emotions! You're always trying to make me feel some other way than what I'm feeling!"

I snap. "Well, excuse me! I thought you wanted to take a bath."

"I do! Dammit!"

"So fuck me for helping you? Shut up and go take a fucking bath!"

I know it's no way to talk to a sick person. I know she's really under a lot of psychological strain...after all, her life is threatened, and she feels bad physically. It's the only time I've ever lost my temper with her, and oddly enough, it seems to work. She takes a bath...then complains afterward that the water wasn't hot enough.

The next day I take Phoebe to the doctor to have the tube removed. That big plastic hose has been sticking out of the side of her ribcage all this time. We go to a doctor's office in a big medical building. Her surgeon, who's a smart, charming man from India, basically grabs the tube and yanks it out. It happens fast. Phoebe looks shocked. The sensation of the tube sliding through her innards makes her queasy. She's left with a hole in the side of her torso that has to be carefully cleaned until it heals.

Besides dealing with these emotional upheavals, I'm trying to stay in touch with my business contacts in Los Angeles. I need to land some paying work soon, and I don't want Marsha Mason to forget about reading my screenplay. At Phoebe's request, I keep track of all my phone calls, so I can reimburse her for them. Part of me feels that this is tightfisted of her. After all, I walked away from my life solely to help her in a time of great need. It seems like she might help me out with phone calls home, but I understand that she's worried about the expenses of this catastrophic illness.

I need to go back to my life, earn some money and take care of myself. Phoebe's handling the chemo well enough that she wants to try going back to work part-time. Joaquin has offered to drive her to her weekly chemo treatments. I feel like she'll be able to get along without me. She agrees. I promise to come back during Easter week and help her plant the garden.

I call Joseph to let him know I'm going back to L.A. I tell him

Phoebe's garden is ready to be planted and how I see that as a metaphor for her healing. He says, "That's good. To be alive in this reality, we must keep moving, materializing ideas and breathing. If we stop any one of those things, we will die physically."

Phoebe takes me to the airport. As we wait at the gate, she thanks me.

"Marsha, this is going to sound weird."

"That's OK. Say it anyway."

"I had the time of my life."

"That is weird. How so?"

"I don't know. I feel so alive now."

"It was a roller coaster ride."

"Yeah...but there's more to it than that."

"You created a miracle."

"I guess I did."

Phoebe is far from healed, but she's alive. We're high on the thrill of that triumph. On the plane, I write in my journal: "What an adventure! I tried my wings as a healer with Joseph coaching me. I was offered the opportunity to create a miracle, and the miracle was created through cooperation. A community coalesced around Phoebe. She transformed from angry, resentful and closed to joyful, alive and open. I experienced my own healing on many levels. I realize now that this cancer killed my mother because she never found the courage to change. I know now that as long as I keep changing, I will be alive. Phoebe gave me the opportunity to know my own courage, love, vitality and strength. Now I see how alive I am."

When I get home, there's a message from Marsha Mason on my answering machine. I call her back.

"I read your screenplay. I loved it. It's the most original thing I've read."

"Wow, thanks."

"I want to option it."

"Great!"

"My lawyer will call you."

I hang up and whisper a prayer of gratitude to my hummingbird.

## CHAPTER 12

# PILGRIMAGE TO RESURRECTION

I get a job on a TV sitcom. My financial situation improves. Marsha Mason's lawyer calls. I put him in touch with my lawyer. A month passes, and they're still talking. The option isn't signed. The sitcom goes on hiatus for Easter Week, and I fly back to Albuquerque to be with Phoebe.

It's going to be a busy week. On the agenda is planting the garden, throwing a birthday party for Phoebe and walking to Chimayo with Joseph. Chimayo is a town in northern New Mexico between Santa Fe and Taos. There's an old church there where the dirt from the floor is supposed to have miraculous healing powers. People come and take a little of the dirt. I'm not sure how they use it. Do they ingest it? Apply it topically? Or just use it as a focus for prayer? Anyway, when they're healed, they bring their crutches or splints or catheter tubes back to the sanctuary and leave them there. The whole place is full of used medical paraphernalia. There's also a little statue of a toddler Christ Child dressed like a doll in a white gown and homemade shoes. The parishioners make new shoes for the statue every year because the old ones get worn out. They say he goes out and walks around at night healing people. During Easter Week, people from all over northern New Mexico walk from their homes to Chimayo as a pilgrimage. The pilgrims all arrive at the church on Good Friday. They stand in line for hours to spend a few moments in the sanctuary. The sleepy town overflows with festivities. Joseph walks the fifty miles from Bernalillo to

Chimayo every year. He usually invites a few of his students to join him. This year, he invites me. I accept without hesitation. I dedicate my walk to Phoebe's healing. If she can endure months of chemotherapy, I can walk 50 miles to support her. The walk is spread out over three days. At night, cars take us back home so we can sleep in our own beds. The next day, they take us back to where we left off the night before. How hard can it be?

Phoebe's birthday is April 16. She's planning a "re-birthday" party to celebrate her new lease on life. She needs my help to pull off the party. Her energy level is low, and she's never given a party before. I'm happy to help. I love the "re-birthday" idea. She's materializing ideas and moving forward.

Phoebe picks me up at the airport. She's wearing a hat to hide her thinning hair. A plastic tube blooms from her chest. She tapes it down between her breasts to keep it out of her way between chemo sessions. As soon as we arrive at her house, she shows me the backyard. A flagstone path meanders across the cultivated soil. She enlisted the help of a friend who's a landscape designer to help her create a plan. The flagstone path was part of it. She had the flagstone delivered. Another friend came to bring her some marijuana to ease her chemo side effects. They both got stoned and Phoebe's friend laid the whole path in one afternoon. It looks good.

Phoebe gives me a list of all the plants she wants to buy for the garden. We look up nurseries in the Yellow Pages. I suggest that we plan the party for the end of the week so we'll have time to prepare and the guests will have as much notice as possible. By now, Phoebe's hair is coming out by the handfuls, and she's anxious about how she's going to look at the party. She considers buying a wig but decides against it. She brings out all of her scarves, and we experiment with different head wraps and turbans. I come up with some pretty sophisticated looks. She admits they look good on her, but she can't quite get past feeling odd about being the only one in a turban. I say, "It's your party. Why not ask all the guests to come with their hair covered up so you'll feel more comfortable?" That's what she does. We sit down together, address the invitations and make a list of what we need for the party. In my uber-efficient way, I integrate the locations of the nurseries with the stops we have to make for party supplies, so we can take the shortest possible route without backtracking. We go out and pick up everything we need for the garden and the party in a couple of hours. While we're shopping at a nursery, Phoebe runs into a friend she hasn't seen in months. When the woman politely asks Phoebe how she is, Phoebe responds, "I have cancer." The woman is flustered. She says, "Oh, I'm so sorry to hear that." Phoebe says, "You don't understand. It's a good thing. I've never felt so alive." I feel a rush of pride and admiration. She's really getting it. She's going to be all right.

When we get back, I cut Phoebe's remaining hair into a short pixie-ish style that will be easy to cover with a scarf. I tell her I was impressed with her positive attitude during the exchange with the woman at the nursery. She says, "It's weird, but I'm really grateful for the cancer." I'm sure she'll be healed.

The next day is the first day of the walk to Chimayo. We start out from Joseph's place in Bernalillo at 6 a.m. I'm wearing expensive new walking shoes. I carry a backpack with water, some apples and a peanut butter sandwich. We walk through the stark beauty of the desert. Our instructions are to stay in silence while we're walking. It quickly becomes obvious that the walking is an extended meditation. Without the distraction of conversation, my mind fills with repetitive chatter. After a couple of hours, it begins to empty until it settles into riding the gentle rhythm of putting one foot in front of the other. The heat of the sun fills the air with the fragrance of juniper and little-leaf sage. Pebbles crunch underfoot. When the hard black highway cuts across our path, we follow it north. Eighteen-wheelers whiz by inches away blasting us with grit and toxic exhaust. Hispanic motorists cheer us with encouraging *gritos*. By now, the sun is blaring straight down. The sizzling asphalt feels like it's frying my feet. We stop for lunch in the shade of a cottonwood tree beside an old abandoned diner. My feet are throbbing. I eat my sandwich without saying a word. It gives me enough energy to continue. I have to pee. There's no restroom for miles. The sparse scrub brush offers no cover. I find a little ravine and squat. I let my skirt drop like a little tent to create some privacy. My urine squirts onto dry grasses that cause it to spray in every direction…all over my khaki skirt. Now I smell like sweat and piss.

We walk on. Every step is painful. I'm beginning to question whether walking beside roaring traffic while breathing serious air pollution can be a spiritual experience. I'd envisioned a romantic hike through the majestic desert. This is not that. By mid-afternoon, I'm physically exhausted and just plain cranky, but because we're walking in silence, I can't complain about it. I walk a short distance behind Joseph. He has an odd, uneven gait because one leg is slightly shorter than the other. Walking this distance with such an out-of-balance anatomy could certainly cause severe back problems. Joseph is close to 60. I tell myself that if Joseph can do it, so can I. That inner dialogue is the only thing that keeps me going. At one point, we stop to rest in a square of shade from a freeway overpass. Joseph asks me about Phoebe's health. I break my silence. I say she seems to be doing well. I tell him what she said about being grateful for the cancer. I add that I'm walking for her. He doesn't comment. As we stand to resume our trek, he says, "She should make three hundred tobacco bundles and bury them."

As the sun sets, we walk up a freeway off ramp to find the support people with cars who will take us home for the night. I take off my shoes. My socks have to be peeled away. My feet are a horrifying sight. They are rubbed raw. The ball of each foot is one huge water blister. Clear fluid oozes out with each agonizing step. I try standing, sitting and walking. My feet burn like they are being held to a flame.

What's really strange is that Joseph's feet are in the same condition. He has the same huge water blisters and raw wounds. He is in the same excruciating pain. Others in the group have sores and blisters to a lesser degree, but Joseph and I are seriously wounded. He's walked the same route every year for thirty odd years and never suffered anything like this before. We've walked eighteen miles. I can't walk another step.

When I get back to Phoebe's, I take a hot bath. I tell myself if I get a good night's sleep, I'll wake up healed and continue the pilgrimage. After all, I'm doing this for someone else's benefit. Surely, my unselfish spiritual motives mean that I'll be able to fulfill my intention.

When the sun comes up, I can barely move. There's no way that I can continue walking. I call Joseph. He says he's in the same shape. He's going to have to ride in a car while the others walk behind him. I ask if I should ride along with him.

"No. Stay there and let Phoebe take care of you."

"I feel like a wimp and a failure."

"How do you think I feel? I'm supposed to be the Big Medicine Man."

We both laugh. He asks me what I think we're supposed to learn from this.

"I think it's about being vulnerable."

"Yes. Letting others see that we're vulnerable."

Phoebe isn't thrilled with the idea of taking care of me. She also doesn't seem particularly appreciative that I wounded myself while making a sacrifice dedicated to her healing. She lapses into anxiety about whether we'll be able to pull off the party and get the garden planted. I rest for a day, then her anxiety prods me to hobble around on my ravaged feet.

I tell Phoebe about the tobacco bundles. The idea is similar to throwing tobacco into the fire before the sweatlodge. You take a pinch of tobacco, blow your intention into it four times and place it in the middle of a small square of cloth. You bring the four corners of the cloth together and wrap them with thread. The result looks like a miniature hobo's bundle. I've seen tobacco bundles strung together to make a necklace worn in the sweatlodge or during a ceremony. Sometimes strings of tobacco bundles are wrapped around a venerable old tree as an offering or to create an outdoor altar. The bundles may be buried or tossed into the fire before or after a sweatlodge. The color of the cloth refers to the medicine wheel. Different colors have different significance. In Joseph's system, yellow represents mental healing and intellectual issues, white represents emotional healing and issues of the heart, black represents physical healing and issues of prosperity, red represents spiritual healing and religious issues. Joseph says tobacco is used because Native Americans smoke as a form of prayer. Smoke makes the breath visible which concretizes the life force. Smoke carries the prayerful intention skyward to the home of Great Spirit. The function of ceremony is to make abstract metaphysical and spiritual ideas concrete so we can grasp them more readily. As a concrete form of life force, tobacco is given as a gift to honor an esteemed person or to show respect. Traditionally, a person seeking healing brings a gift of tobacco to the shaman. Joseph also taught us to give an offering of tobacco to a plant to show our gratitude when we harvest part of it for food or medicine.

Phoebe listens to my whole explanation about tobacco bundles. She says she'll make them, but I can tell it's low on her list of priorities. The immediate priority is planting the garden. We have the plants. We have the plan. It's a toss-up as far as who's in worse physical shape. Phoebe's battling nausea, anxiety and low energy. I can hardly walk.

I plant the garden. She helps me place the plants where she wants them. I get down on my hands and knees to dig the holes, knock the plants out of their pots, put them in the earth, fill in the dirt and water. She rests. It takes a whole day. I enjoy the work. I love having my hands in the earth. I love the pungent smell of herbs and oily leaves. I love being outside under the incredible New Mexico sky with its towering clouds and crystal blue vastness. Gardening is another form of meditation. It's easy to focus on the sensuous moment of the task. All the chatter falls out of my head. On this particular day, being on my hands and knees is much preferable to being on my feet. When the job is done, I feel a deep sense of satisfaction...almost deep enough to counter the devastating sense of failure I feel from not being able to finish the walk to Chimayo. Phoebe comes out to inspect my work. Her unspoken reaction is a mix of relief and joy. She thanks me. A couple of months ago, she thought this task was impossible. We've accomplished a small miracle.

I take a hot shower. She pours glasses of cold white wine. We sit on a garden bench and sip the wine at twilight. Crickets begin to sing. An elegant crescent moon eases over the horizon. Very few words pass between us. Anxieties are forgotten for a moment. We are in communion.

The party is the next evening. I can barely walk. Phoebe's house needs cleaning. Furniture needs rearranging. Tables need setting. There's a lot of work to be done and none of it can be done on hands and knees, so there's no way I can do it all. Once that becomes obvious, Phoebe kicks into gear. She runs on sheer adrenaline. She cleans the house. We move furniture together. I ice the drinks, set up the bar and buffet table. Thankfully, it's potluck, so we didn't have to cook. She picks up a monster-size cheesecake that she ordered to be her "re-birthday" cake. I set out chips and snacks. We shower and dress…and fret over how to cover our hair. She tries several hats and scarves before settling on a chic turban with ornate dangle earrings. I tie a scarf in various ways and finally opt for an Aunt-Jemima-style wrap with some faux chilies tied into the knot. We compliment each other on looking pretty cute. We pose for photos and pour ourselves glasses of wine.

The doorbell rings. Phoebe opens the door to the first guest. Love pours into the house. At least twenty people show up…in cowboy hats, baseball hats, straw hats, ski caps and scarves tied every which way. Conviviality and conversation fill the living room, the patios and the newly planted garden. The buffet table overflows with incredible food. Gifts are stacked in every corner. People toast Phoebe's health and sing "Happy Birthday." Everyone knows what Phoebe wishes for when she blows out the candles. She shares the giant cheesecake with her guests. Her nausea has vanished completely. She eats and drinks everything in sight. Phoebe opens an abundance of gifts. I give her a necklace and earrings of deep green malachite, the precious stone of the Goddess.

I look out at a room packed with people wearing silly things on their heads. The universal willingness to support Phoebe's healing process...even if it means looking foolish or feeling uncomfortable...touches me deeply. Phoebe doesn't need me. She has healing angels all around her. She just never noticed them before. At last, she's invited love into her life. Phoebe gives a prize for the best-covered head. It goes to Rosa, who figured out how to tie a scarf so that it covered every bit of hair. She wins a jester's cap. I congratulate her and thank her again for all she's done to help. She says, "Don't take this the wrong way, but you're not what I expected."

"What did you expect?"

"I thought you'd be a rich, glamorous blonde from Hollywood." I laugh.

"Couldn't have been further from the truth. I'm not rich or glamorous...and I'm only blonde to cover the gray." She laughs too.

"I was pleasantly surprised."

The re-birthday party is successful beyond our highest hopes.

Phoebe is so giddy after the guests leave that even cleaning up is fun. I know Phoebe has taken an important step toward healing herself.

The next day is Easter Sunday. I've booked a session with Phoebe's breathwork therapist in search of my own private resurrection. I've never done breathwork before. As I understand it, the therapist guides you to do a certain kind of breathing that causes you to enter an altered state. Many people relive their birth experience. The therapist helps the client deal with negative issues around being born to make it a more positive experience than it was the first time. Phoebe felt it helped her and encouraged me to try it. I'm willing to give it a whirl.

I go to a suburban tract house on the western edge of Albuquerque. Patty Brooks greets me at the front door. She's a warm, motherly woman who explains that her husband will take her two girls to the park while we work. The house is decorated in that cute ruffled country style. Toys are everywhere. She introduces her husband and two darling girls...maybe five and seven...as they're going out the door. She tells me to lie down on my back on the living room floor and instructs me to breathe with rapid, shallow pants. When we were kids, we used to do something similar to get high by hyperventilating. Well, guess what? It does make you high. Whenever my panting slows down, Patty urges me on. Breathing is starting to feel like a lot of work. I begin to feel dizzy. The room seems to tip from side to side. I see stars against a background of changing colors...deep blue fading into purple and mauve. Without warning, waves of energy start pulsing through my body. They radiate out from my solar plexus in concentric circles. I recognize that this is "chi", the body's electrical energy that I'd felt before during Tai Chi and Chi Gong. I'd felt it before, but never this strongly...and it's getting more intense with each wave. The effect is something like a non-sexual orgasm. The waves of energy get so intense that I'm paralyzed. The energy is so strong that it pins me to the floor. When the intensity starts to dissipate, the sensation of being born begins. I feel like I'm being forced out of a safe, warm place into claustrophobic darkness. Then I'm dumped into a bright unknown. I fight to breathe again while Patty cradles me in her arms and tells me everything is all right. She rocks me like a baby.

When I get back to Phoebe's, I'm exhausted and relaxed. She asks me about the session. I tell her about being paralyzed by the waves of chi. She says nothing that dramatic ever happened to her. I sleep in a hammock under her pecan tree for the rest of the afternoon.

In the evening, Phoebe gets on an arts and crafts kick. It's Easter, so she wants to make Ukrainian eggs. I've never made them before, but she took a class and has all this equipment. It's a wax-resist process. You melt wax and draw intricate designs on the eggs with it by using this special little tool that's like a spoon with a tiny funnel extending from the bowl. You dip the egg in various dyes adding more designs after each color. It seems like a hell of a lot of work, but Phoebe's all excited about it, so I'm game. She puts on a tape with all of our favorite music from our college days...Rolling Stones, Steely Dan, Cream, Joni Mitchell and, of course, Bob Dylan. We smoke a couple of joints as we melt the wax, put newspapers on the table and set up the dyes. By the time we get down to doing eggs, I'm way too stoned to be able to execute the precise hand-to-eye coordination necessary to lay down a straight line of hot liquid on a curved surface. The little spoon zigs and zags, stutters and splatters as I try to follow the rounded shape. I get the giggles. Phoebe catches them from me. We try to stop laughing to keep from messing up our eggs. It's hopeless. We smoke some more and sing along with the classic oldies. My eggs turn out more Jackson Pollack than Russian Orthodox. Phoebe's are only marginally more presentable, but we have a blast.

I fly home the next day. Phoebe says it's a good thing I'm going home because she isn't getting enough rest. She complains that none of her friends ever call her when I'm not there.

"How do you know they're not calling? You don't have an answering machine. They could be calling when you're at chemo or your cancer support group or when you unplug the phone while you're napping. Get an answering machine."

Phoebe almost cries when we say goodbye at the airport, and so do I. "La Muerta" is still looking over our shoulders, but we've defied her by packing a lot of life into a few days. When I get off the plane in L.A., I'm still limping.

The lawyers finally finish negotiating. Marsha Mason and I sign an option agreement for my screenplay. She gives me a check for $5,000 and I give her the rights for a year. She tells me she sold her luxury home in Pacific Palisades and is moving to a ranch…near Santa Fe.

Phoebe gets an answering machine. Her ex-husband's mother, who's still a close friend years after the divorce, sends it to her as a re-birthday gift.

## CHAPTER 13

# DRUM DANCE

Phoebe's social life does pick up after she gets the answering machine. Her recovery picks up too. The doctors add radiation treatments to the chemotherapy. She loses every bit of hair, but in September, she's officially declared cancer-free.

Celebration is in order. Phoebe suggests that I make another trip to join her in an excursion to Ojo Caliente so we can soak in the hot springs and indulge ourselves with massages and herbal wraps. I tell Marsha Mason I'm going to be in New Mexico. She invites me to stay at her ranch and work on revising the screenplay. When I call Joseph to tell him that Phoebe is cured, he reminds me that the Drum Dance is scheduled while I'm planning to be there.

"You need to dance," he says simply. As far as I'm concerned, he brought Phoebe back from the dead. If he says, "dance," I'll dance. I tell him to count me in. Soon after that, I find out there's more to the dance than just dancing. It's three days of dancing to the drums in silence…with no food…and no water. According to Joseph, this "dry fast" changes the body's chemistry in a way that allows the brain to make a radical leap to a higher state of consciousness. The idea sounds a little crazy. Three days with no water can't possibly be good for the kidneys…even if it does facilitate spiritual enlightenment. I wrecked my feet on the first day of the walk to Chimayo. I'm afraid I'll do a lot of damage to myself during three days of dancing and dry fasting in the desert…that is if I make it through three whole days. I wiped out of the Chimayo walk after one day, and I was eating and drinking during that one. Once I understand what the Drum Dance entails, I doubt that I have what it will take. As soon as I get to New Mexico, I go see Joseph to talk about my fears and see if I can back out of my commitment. He assures me that my spiritual intention will protect me from physical harm. I tell him that I feel like such a failure from the Chimayo experience, that I'm afraid that this will just waste my time…and his. He says that no effort is a waste of time. He gives me permission to do as much as I can.

"It's best if you don't take a drink of water until the dance is over. If you do, it undoes what you've accomplished, but you'll get a lot out of it anyway."

"Why am I doing this?"

"You're giving up food and water for three days as a sacrifice to give thanks for the healing, to achieve insight and to promote world peace."

"Should I dedicate my dance to Phoebe?"

"No. This dance is your medicine. This is about you replenishing yourself. You must renew your own medicine before you continue to help others."

"What does this have to do with world peace?"

"When you deepen your inner peace, you add to world peace."

About twenty dancers meet at Joseph's at seven in the morning. His brothers, Benito and Tayo, arrived from Picuris the night before. They're drummers who will provide the steady heartbeat of our dance. We caravan out to Pecos. From there, we follow a narrow, winding road into the mountains. We turn off on a dirt road that leads into private property. We stop while Benito unlocks a gate, so we can pass through a barbed wire fence. He locks it again when all the cars are inside. We've left civilization behind us. On this vast acreage are tall pines, lush meadows and open sky. The high altitude means temperatures are cool enough that a few wildflowers are still in bloom even though summer is nearly over. We park next to the only remnants of human habitation: a dilapidated log cabin and a rickety outhouse. This land belongs to the heirs of Robert Oppenheimer. During the years when the atom bomb was being developed at Los Alamos, this place was a summer retreat where overworked scientists sipped white wine and listened to chamber music in the meadows. Now the family allows spiritual groups to use it for healing ceremonies as a way of atoning for the ugly karma kicked up by the scientists' destructive brainchildren.

In indigenous cultures, dance is not a performance. Rather it's a deep meditation for the dancer. Rhythm and movement are often repetitive in order to induce trance. Village dances, like the ones practiced by Native American pueblo cultures, create group trance with a focused positive intention. The dance is not about form or choreography. Dancers include grandmothers, children and everyone in between. All dancers move at their own level of ability and in their own style. The experience is internal. There is no audience.

For our dance, Joseph strings a rope between two trees about 50 feet apart. He ties painted feathers to the rope...one feather every 2 or 3 feet. He tells us to set up our tents and sleeping bags in a row about 20 feet from the rope. Benito and Tayo build a little tarp-covered shelter for their big pow-wow drum. When the drumming starts, we are to dance from our tent up to the rope and back without ever taking our eyes off the feathers. We're to keep dancing as long as the drummers are playing. Over three days, our steps will wear a path in the grass that's symbolic of the path that we create for ourselves in life. We're to stay in silence at all times. The only time we can leave our dance path is to use the outhouse.

After the explanation, Joseph tells us to get ready to sweat. The fire was started when we first arrived, and the rocks are almost ready. We dress in our sweat clothes and hike down a hill to the sweatlodge. We sit outside until Joseph invites us in. By now, the womb-like darkness is so familiar to me that it feels like home. The smell of the sage and cedar smoke rising off the hot rocks is as comforting as the smell of coffee brewing in the morning. I've truly embraced the heat. I drink in the sizzling steam. Dancers pray for strength and guidance. They pray for personal healing and world peace. Joseph exhorts us to keep those goals in mind when the going gets rough and we want to quit. At the end of the fourth round, he tells us our dry fast has begun. We are to go back to our tents, dress in our ceremonial clothes and wait for the drums to call us.

Usually the fourth round of a sweatlodge is immediately followed by a plunge into a mountain lake, a bracing rinse with a garden hose, a bite of juicy watermelon or at least a tall cool glass of water. Not this time. The sweatlodge leaves us thoroughly dehydrated, and we're on our honor not to touch water for three days.

Ceremonial clothes are an expression of each dancer's individuality. The only requirement is that both men and women wear skirts. As I understand it, the lower chakras need to be open to the energy of the earth, and pants interfere with that flow of energy. Men wear long apron-like wraps or sarongs. Women wear chaste long skirts and tops with modest necklines and sleeves. Some dancers have created elaborate outfits decorated with personal spiritual symbols. There are deerskin dresses, fringed shawls, ribbon shirts. Some dancers dress simply but respectfully. Some dancers have a different outfit for each of the three days. I wear a loose turquoise blouse over a long full skirt in a blue and turquoise print. On my right, an African-American woman, who's dancing to celebrate her tenth year of sobriety, is dressed in a flowing robe and head wrap of pure white. On my left, an East Indian man wears a Nehru jacket over a matching sarong. We wait in silence for over an hour. Finally, Benito and Tayo appear and settle into plastic chairs beside the big drum. Joseph strolls up and gives them a nod.

Boom! Boom! Boom! They strike the drum in unison with leather-padded sticks. Their voices blend in some ancient wailing chant. The drumsticks fall in rhythm with my heartbeat. The vibrations thrill me. The pulsing sounds lift my feet for me as I move toward my feather. I dance! My mind is in my feet. My eyes are on the feather. My heart is one with the drum. I move with no effort. It's easy and fun. We dance for about two hours. When the drums stop, Joseph tells us to go back to our tents and rest until the drums call us again. I sit on my sleeping bag for about an hour. The drums start again. I scramble to my feet, grab my rattles and dance for another couple of hours. We rest and dance three or four more times. The last dance is well after dark. Joseph tells us the drums will call us again in the morning.

When I fall asleep, my stomach is growling with hunger and I'm thirsty. That night, I dream about food and drink. Visions of juicy papayas and tangy mangos dance in my head. I can feel my lips sipping from a frosty glass of cranberry juice tinkling with crushed ice. I lick creamy sweet yogurt from a cool silver spoon.

The drums call us before dawn. Three loud beats wake me from a sound sleep. I fumble to pull myself together enough to dance. Other dancers are doing the same. When we are all lined up, Joseph tells us to face east. Benito and Tayo begin to sing a flowing, melodic song. The words sound like "Way-oh, way-oh" and repeat over and over. It's a hypnotic chant. Eventually we all join in. The drums are silent. As we sing, we watch the eastern sky. Darkness gives way to a pale blue glow. Then a pink streak outlines the horizon. After about 15 minutes of mesmerizing singing, the sun peeks out at us.

"Sing the sun up," Joseph encourages us. We sing with new energy. The sun hears our voices and responds by steadily rising into the sky. It's a moment of being magically melded with nature. We all glow like rising suns.

We dance and rest, dance and rest, dance and rest. The monotonous drumbeat becomes an enforced meditation. There's no way to think about anything while you dance. There are no distractions to escape into while you rest. There's nowhere to go except deep inside yourself.

By mid-day, I forget my hunger…mainly because I'm obsessed with my thirst. My body is crying out for water. My lips are sticking to my teeth. My tongue is sticking to the inside of my mouth. My throat aches. I'm light-headed and unsteady on my feet. The last time I tried to pee, nothing came out. My head's filled with questions about how long a person can live without water. Is it four days? Or three days? What happens to your kidneys when there's no water flowing through them? Your bladder? Your mucus membranes? Am I doing damage to myself? Am I being an idiot for doing this? This isn't fun anymore.

That afternoon, Joseph stops the dancing and tells us to look at our hands. He explains that the shape of the hand is a spiritual metaphor to Native Americans.

"The little finger represents polarity. That's when we feel separate from others or in opposition to something. The ring finger represents reconciliation, our urge to bring opposites together. The middle finger represents unity, the state where opposites have merged into one. The index finger represents our purpose. When we have passed through all these states, we come to the thumb. It represents the transformation of our potential. Once we complete this cycle of spiritual growth, we go back to the little finger and start again. When you see the outline of a hand in petroglyphs or on a warrior's shield, that's what it means."

Joseph has a way of speaking that almost lulls me to sleep. I find it impossible to analyze what he's saying with any intellectual acuteness. I always worry that I'm not going to remember important concepts. Apparently, the effect is intentional. It allows information to enter consciousness through some door other than intellect.

I look at my hands. I feel like I have talents, abilities and ideas that are sadly unrealized. I want to transform my potential. Where am I in the cycle? Pinky? Ring finger? I know I'm a long way from thumb. The incentive of transforming my potential spurs me on despite my discomfort. My skin prickles with dryness. My throat feels like it's about to split open. My thick sticky tongue is gagging me. My muscles ache with every movement, but some odd lust to become the person I know I have the potential to be overwhelms my fear of physical injury. My now-addled brain tells me I can risk it. I healed my feet after Chimayo. I can heal whatever I need to heal after this. I dance on into twilight.

The insistent staccato beat of the drums stops abruptly. Joseph, Benito and Tayo turn toward the line of feathers. They began to sing a soft lilting song. Their voices ring like bells as darkness descends. In response to this gentle love song, a huge pearly full moon slips up from behind the mountain and hangs just above the line of feathers. Her shining silvery face smiles down on us so lovingly that I begin to cry, but there are no tears.

That night, I dream of rain. I dream of a gentle drizzle that creates sparkling drops in the long grass. Leaves collect crystal teaspoons of clear fresh water. I tip each leaf into my mouth and drink from it. I feel guilty immediately because I'm cheating. I wonder if those few delicious sips will really undo all I've accomplished. I wonder if drinking in the dreamtime is a violation of the vow.

I wake from the dream. My tent is dark. The ground is hard. A rock is digging into my back. I hurt all over. My dream tantalizes me. My thirst is more than I can bear. I fumble for my water bottle in the dark. I find it. As I'm unscrewing the cap, I hear a whispering patter. I smell moisture in the air. I realize it's raining in reality. I put down my water and climb out of my tent. I stand on the moist earth with my bare feet. I turn my face up and let the gentle drizzle kiss my skin. I open my mouth and let a few drops fall on my tongue. This isn't cheating. This is accepting a natural blessing from Great Spirit.

The rain stops. I look down and blink with surprise. I see something I've never seen before. My own shadow is a crisp, dark outline against the earth...in the middle of the night. My first reaction is that I'm hallucinating, then I look up at the sky. The full moon is shining with such intensity that the whole night is softly illuminated. Moonshadows are falling everywhere.

I sit outside for the rest of the night lost in the soothing dampness of this enchanted world. I rest in the blessings of mist and moonlight. This time, I'm ready when the drums call us before dawn. My voice joins the chorus that sings the sun up. I summon all my energy and attack the first dance with enthusiasm. I'm determined to keep dancing for one more day.

In spite of my good intentions, my energy fades fast. By mid-morning, I'm fighting to stay on my feet. I'm obsessed with my thirst. My dance is reduced to an unsteady shuffle. I study the position of the sun and try to calculate how much longer I have to endure until I can pour water down my throat. I look down and see my hand. My head clears, and Joseph's teaching floats into my consciousness as I dance. Polarity...I've experienced that. I've been in opposition to my husband, to men in general, to death and disease. Reconciliation...I've felt that. I've wanted to make peace with all those opposing things. Unity...I'm getting there. Now I see that my divorce and my parents' deaths were great teachers for me. I see that disease is motivating growth for Phoebe. I understand that I'm part of all those things I've battled against. I stare at my index finger. What was next?

Joseph whispers in my ear, "Purpose." What's my purpose? I turn the question over in my mind a few times. I decide that my purpose is no purpose. My purpose is simply to embrace life and live as me in all my complexity and imperfection. The realization energizes me. I dance with new vigor. Only then, do I realize that

Joseph is nowhere near me. He's standing under the drum shelter with his brothers. I'm dancing about 70 feet away. There's no way he could have whispered in my ear, but I heard his voice clearly. The word he spoke was the answer to a specific question in my mind. Maybe it was an auditory hallucination brought on by dehydration. Maybe it was my imagination. Maybe it was a ventriloquist's trick coupled with mental telepathy. Maybe Joseph was actually inside my head. Whatever it was, it did trigger a sudden shift in my consciousness.

When the sun is straight overhead, Joseph unties the rope from one of the trees and starts gathering it up as he walks to the other tree. The drums continue to play. We continue to dance. When he gets to the other tree and unties the rope, the drumming stops. The dance is over. He tells us to go stand by our tents. We stand in a line facing where the feathers used to be. A path of flattened grass stretches out in front of each dancer.

"Look at the path you made as you danced. This is your path in life. You make it with your actions, with your energy, with your intention. Be proud of your creation."

Joseph takes his magnificent eagle feather fan and walks behind the line of dancers. He stops and touches each person on the back. When the great wing brushes me between the shoulder blades, energy surges from my solar plexus. It feels like somebody threw a switch. My power is turned on. My fatigue disappears. I made it! I endured the difficulties! I passed the spiritual test! I can fly with eagles!

One by one, Joseph asks each of us to walk out to the middle of our path and kneel on the earth. He takes a glass of water and pours it over each dancer's head. He refills the glass and invites the dancer to drink. Finally, it's my turn. I walk proudly and sink to my knees on my well-worn path. I know every rock and stick and stubborn weed along those few feet of earth. It's comfortable to put my body on such familiar ground. The cold water shocks my senses as it splashes on my scalp, soaks into my hair, runs around my ears and trickles down my neck. Then Joseph presents me with a glass of water as though it's the medal of honor.

"Congratulations. Drink this slowly."

I sip. Nothing ever tasted so good. It's like sweet silver soothing my mouth and sliding down my suffering throat. It's more intoxicating than the finest wine. It's even more delicious than the stolen sips in my dream. I hold every gulp in my mouth to savor the miraculous taste. Drinking a glass of water is an ordinary act in my mundane life. At this moment, it's transformed into a sacred rite. This is a high communion with life.

Our glasses are refilled. We're handed slices of the sweetest, juiciest watermelon ever grown on earth. Joseph tells us to stay in silent meditation for the next half hour. Then we're to walk down to the cabin for a feast.

It takes half an hour to gather enough strength to walk down the hill. Outside the cabin, tables are brimming with food: watermelon, strawberries, bananas, oranges, bread, cheese, chips and salsa, trail mix and even beef stew. Most tempting to me are the bottles of juice. I put ice in my glass and fill it up with cranberry juice. I swallow the frosty sweet-tart liquid. My dream comes true.

Our stomachs are too traumatized to allow us to eat much, but the feast also marks the breaking of our silence. We sample food, drink juice and share our experience with fellow dancers. The food grounds us in ordinary reality. When I've regained my strength, I pack up my tent, say "Goodbye" to Joseph, his brothers and new friends...and drive back to Albuquerque.

It's impossible to explain the dance to Phoebe. The experiential lesson is beyond words. Now I know what Joseph means by "cellular change". The teaching impacts every cell, so it's not something you can just forget, but trying to share the experience with a non-combatant is like trying to tell a stranger about rock 'n roll.

Phoebe is skeptical, and her patience is limited. Although she's cancer free, and the plastic tube has been removed from her chest, she's still uncomfortable. She's lost every bit of hair and feels self-conscious about it. All the Haagen Dazs she ate during chemo left her plump. She's working with a nutritionist who has her on a strict anti-cancer and weight-loss diet. She's not allowed to eat the things she loves. I can't even keep track of all the forbidden foods. She's cranky and short-tempered. I feel guilty about eating in front of her, even though I'm recovering from three days of fasting.

I'm glad we're going to Ojo Caliente, primarily because I can't wait to immerse myself in WATER! I'm also hoping that soaking in the hot springs will relax Phoebe and make it a little easier to be with her. I give her a gift to honor her for successfully healing herself. It's a white sweatshirt with an image of a playful cat, a one-of-kind work of art hand painted by a Chinese calligrapher. It's an expensive gift, but I want to show Phoebe that's she's loved. I also give her a royal blue T-shirt with the Navajo "Walk In Beauty" prayer silk-screened on it. I tell her I got one for myself and sent one each to Tillie and Lenore.

"Now you and your 'healing team' have an official uniform."

"What about Marilyn?"

"What about her?"

"Did you send her a T-shirt?"

"No."

"Why not? She was part of the healing team too."

"I didn't think of it. I'm sorry."

"Well, I hope she doesn't find out. She'll feel really left out. You should have thought of that."

Ojo Caliente is not a luxury spa. That's what I like about it. It's natural hot springs where various pools contain different kinds of minerals...like iron, soda, arsenic and lithia. The ancient Anasazi Indians used these waters for healing. A hotel was built in the late 1800s and has been only slightly remodeled since. It's a funky old lodge with dark woodwork and big stone fireplaces. There are no showers or bathtubs in the rooms, because you do your bathing in the springs. In recent years, a conventional swimming pool has been added and enclosures have been built around some of the pools. Phoebe and I have been here before. It's one of our favorite stops in our travels around New Mexico.

You can spend the day going from pool to pool. Our favorite is the soda pool. It's an enclosed rock grotto, so it's always semi-dark. The pool has a natural sand floor and the hot water comes up through the sand. It's very hot in some places and lukewarm in others, so you change the temperature by moving around. It's big enough to swim a few strokes. There are separate enclosures for men and women, so you can bathe nude in the safe, earthy atmosphere of a Goddess shrine. (In recent years, the sand floor has been covered with concrete and all the pools have been opened to men and women. Today, bathing suits are required.)

After soaking in the various pools, you retire to the bathhouse where you lie down on a cot. An attendant wraps you in a cotton sheet and then a wool blanket. You lie still like a mummy for about half an hour and sweat. Toxins pour out of your body. Then you shower off and proceed to whatever massage or facial or herbal wrap treatment that you've booked...or take a delicious nap until time for dinner.

During this visit, my heart breaks as I watch Phoebe slip into the soda pool. Her bald head is just beginning to sprout some peach fuzz. Her chest and ribs are streaked with vicious blue scars where tubes were inserted and tissue samples were harvested. Her ravaged body makes her pain visible to me. Phoebe soaks for just a few minutes before being stricken with a migraine headache. She retreats to our room and crawls into bed. She stays there with shades drawn and lights out for the duration of our stay. I tiptoe in and change clothes to go to the dining room. I ask if she wants me to bring her some food.

"No. They probably don't have anything I can eat anyway."

I eat grilled trout and crisp salad and indulge in a glass of white wine. I sit by the stone fireplace for a while before I tiptoe back into the room. Phoebe is sound asleep.

On the way back to Albuquerque, we stop at a raspberry farm and buy a lug of fresh raspberries. They are on Phoebe's diet. We've invited Carlos and Joaquin over for dinner. I suggest a raspberry fiesta with raspberries as an ingredient in every course: chicken breasts with raspberry glaze, spinach salad with raspberries and feta cheese, raspberries and ice cream for desert. Phoebe reminds me that she can't eat ice cream. I suggest raspberry tarts. In a martyred tone, she says she'll just eat the raspberries and we can have the ice cream.

Phoebe's still recovering from the migraine, so I do most of the cooking. Joaquin, who is a full-time homemaker while Carlos works, drove Phoebe to every chemotherapy session, waited for her and drove her home. I suggested inviting them to dinner as a gesture of appreciation. They appreciate being appreciated. They're bright, fun dinner guests who enjoy the food, keep us laughing and toast Phoebe's good health. The three of us drink wine. Phoebe sticks with her diet and drinks water. Almost everything else (except the ice cream) is on Phoebe's diet. I congratulate myself for creatively working around severe restrictions. Phoebe clears the table as I prepare desert and make lemon ginger tea to serve with it. We sit down at the table and pick up our spoons. Phoebe takes a sip of her tea and nearly spits. She snaps at me, "I can't have lemon!"

"I'm sorry. I forgot. I'll make some without lemon for you."

"Never mind. I just won't have any."

She pushes back her chair, takes her teacup, storms into the kitchen and dumps the tea in the sink with a flourish.

Carlos, Joaquin and I trade glances, raise our eyebrows and don't say a word. They polish off their deserts quickly and make an abrupt exit.

I move to Marsha Mason's ranch the next day. It's a relief to escape from the tyranny of Phoebe's dark moods, and I'm glad to have Marsha as a sounding board.

"I know it's been really tough for her. I guess I can't expect her to be in a positive mood all the time."

"Maybe not."

"I don't blame her for being cranky…she's on that diet…she

has no hair…"

"She's alive."

"But I think it's good that she's expressing her anger. After what I went through with my mother, I figured out that cancer is about repressed anger. It's progress that she's dealing with it. I just don't like that it gets directed at me…but I guess I'm her most intimate relationship right now."

"But she's not dealing with her anger. She's just using it to beat you up. She's trying to control you and everybody else, so she never has to feel anger. That is not dealing with your anger."

I know Marsha's making an important point, but I'm confused about how to deal with Phoebe. Our pact was that we would take care of each other in times of emergency. I've done my best to keep my part of the bargain. Phoebe seems angry that I haven't done enough. I really want to give her what she needs, but when does my obligation end?

Marsha and I turn our attention to the screenplay. She suggests new ideas and I expand on them. I relax and forget about Phoebe. I swim in Marsha's pool. We harvest vegetables from her garden. I cook lavish vegetarian feasts for us. The collaboration inspires me. I'm excited about going back to L.A. and digging into the rewrite.

I see Phoebe one more time before I leave. She's in a lighter mood. She tells me that she plans to start attending a women's dream circle. I ask her if she ever made the tobacco bundles. She says she hasn't but she still plans to. She invites me back for New Year's and proposes that we try to learn cross-country skiing to celebrate her new lease on life. New year, new lease on life, new sport. I'm up for it.

# CHAPTER 14

# DARK DREAMS

Joseph warned us that the effects of the Drum Dance start before the dance begins and continue long after the dance ends. He told us to pay particular attention to our dreams in the months after the dance. I return to my life in Los Angeles and become a dreaming machine. In one instance, I dream two dreams at the same time.

One dream is set in the "wild west." Two sisters, one blond and one brunette, arrive in a frontier town. They rent a dilapidated old house, clean out all the junk in it, fix it up nicely and move in.

At this point, a dream set in the present "intercuts" with the western-movie dream. I see myself cleaning out the back room of the last house where I lived with my husband. The room was his workshop and artist's studio. I throw away his old junk but save his paintings and stack them neatly in the corner.

Back in the western dream, the two sisters are living happily in their little cottage, but they wish they had men in their lives and don't know how to attract them. Winter comes, and they sit by the fireplace in their house. A narrator's voice says, "Sit by the fire. The fire is purifying. Stay by the fire, and you'll become pure enough to be with another." Suddenly, the sisters are surrounded by all different kinds of men. The blond sister chooses a young, rugged man with dark hair. The dark sister accepts a dinner invitation from a tall blond doctor with wire-rimmed glasses.

In the contemporary dream, my ex-husband is kneeling in front of large painting of me that he did when I was young and the marriage was good. In this painting, I'm sitting in a chair holding an eggplant. In the dream, my husband is about to pound a nail into the painting. I say, "Don't! You'll wreck it." He says, "Don't tell me what to do. I know what I'm doing." He pounds the nail in, and I know he's ruined the painting.

In the western dream, the dark sister and the blond doctor have rented a basement room in a whorehouse. They intend to have sex. They are both fully dressed. He's in a gray suit. She's still wearing her hat. I hear the voice of the madam say, "If there's anything you need, just let me know." The dark sister closes the door and turns to the doctor.

I wake up.

I recognize that this is an important healing dream for me. I've been divorced for six years and haven't had a romantic relationship with a man in all that time. I've had half a dozen one-night stands and a lot of solitude. I've compensated by focusing on inner work and spiritual questing. In the first couple of years after my divorce, whenever I had an erotic dream, the man I was having sex with would turn into my ex-husband. In one dream, I tried to strangle him and told him to stay out of my dreams.

I call Joseph and tell him about the western-movie dream. His first question is "What part of your body did the nail go through?" I say, "My knees." He says, "The knees symbolize completion. You are completing a cycle." He confirms my intuition that the dream is about dark sexual healing and urges me to seek out and confront all types of dark energy, "Invite it to consume you."

The next weeks are dense with deep, difficult psychological work. In the interest of inviting dark sexual energy to consume me, I track down the psychologist who counseled us during the divorce and make an appointment to see her.

She's softened over the years. Now she wears casual sandals instead of high heels. She looks relaxed in a loose-fitting top and pants of dark pink silk. When I ended my therapy with her after my divorce, she told me, "There's nothing wrong with you. You're a woman capable of great love."

I remind her of that and tell her that I haven't been in a serious romantic relationship since my marriage ended. She asks me how Jack survived the divorce. I tell her that he seems unscathed. After initially trying to win me back by sending me flowers (charged to my credit card) and a few idle suicidal threats, he seduced the real estate agent who came to appraise our house when we were considering selling it. She moved in within weeks. We refinanced and I used my half of the equity to buy a house of my own. Although Jack seems to have found happiness with the first woman who walked in the door after I walked out, I'm still struggling with my guilt about abandoning him when he was mentally ill.

The psychologist listens and leads me to the realization that during the year we were in therapy, I was so focused on healing him that I never dealt with the effect of his descent into mental illness on my psyche. She nails the fear that paralyzes me.

"Something that was very precious to you suddenly turned dark and disturbing...and you're afraid that will happen again."

"Yes, I am." I reach for a tissue as tears start to spill down my cheeks.

"Sorry, your hour is up."

In the next weeks, torrents of anger and sadness tear through me. I weep violently. I dream constantly. I slip into depression.

The ceiling falls down in my bedroom. Strange men peer into

the dark hole over my bed and try to figure out what went wrong.

I dream that I'm having sex with Jack. He says, "I have a surprise for you." He puts on women's lingerie...a navy blue Merry Widow, a white garter belt and lacy white stockings. I find it exciting and the lovemaking heats up. I rub myself against him. I'm close to orgasm when I hear the back door of the house open. Fast urgent footsteps approach the bedroom. We both jump out of bed, Jack opens the bedroom door. I hear him and the intruder run outside. I follow them but can't see them. I stand on the back porch thinking, "Oh my God. My husband is running around the neighborhood in women's underwear."

I wake up frightened. My heart is pounding.

Later I remember what Joseph said, "Invite it to consume you." So I go back into the dream in active imagination. I'm not asleep, but I imagine the dream again and take an active role in it. This time when I hear the intruder approach the bedroom, I open the door and confront him. He's a dark shadow man. I invite him to consume me. I realize it's him that I'm really attracted to. He pushes me down on the bed and starts to make love to me. He becomes a black blanket covering me, then he transforms into a snake, enters my vagina and fills me up to my throat. I have a huge orgasm. He transforms back into the black blanket and is absorbed into me.

My ceiling gets repaired. My depression lifts, and I start to feel euphoric. A couple of weeks later, a sweet young man rear-ends me on the freeway. I hit the back of my head on the headrest and bump my knee on the dashboard. I'm not really hurt, but a wave of emotion sweeps through me. I feel like it's some kind of spiritual event.

I work on rewriting the screenplay as Marsha Mason and I had discussed. The ideas work. The story takes on new life.

I get a job as first assistant director on a sitcom being shot in New York. For a month, I share an apartment in Queens with two roommates: the female production coordinator and a gay man who is post-production supervisor of the show. I've worked with them both in past, so it's not like we're strangers. Our work days are so long that we spend very little time in the apartment, but when we're there, we're able to live together harmoniously. We rehearse and shoot one episode. The executive producer and the network get into a squabble over "creative differences," and we're given a day off while they negotiate. I take the subway into Manhattan. I go see a movie, shop at Bloomingdale's and get something to eat. By the time I get back to our office at Kauffman-Astoria Studios, a moving van is parked out in front. The furniture is being moved out of our office into the van. The sitcom has been cancelled. I fly back to Los Angeles the next day.

I call Phoebe to tell her about New York. She tells me that she went to the women's dream circle a couple of times but feels like she doesn't fit in, so she's not going back. I can tell that she thinks I'm going to criticize her decision, so I'm careful to choose words that are non-judgmental.

"Why you feel like you don't fit in is something you can look at."

About a week later, I get a letter from her. It begins, "I've been bothered by your comment that I should 'look at' why I want to quit the dream circle. Why do you disapprove of everything I do? You are always so judgmental. Can't you just accept me the way I am?" She goes on and on for two pages about how critical I am and how I don't allow her to have her own feelings. My comments make her feel discounted and inadequate. She ends by asking me if I think saving the friendship is worth discussing these things.

I call her to discuss these things.

"Phoebe, I don't disapprove of you at all. I think you're doing everything right."

"Yes, you do disapprove of me. I can tell by the tone of your voice. You just refuse to take responsibility for your part in this."

"You're asking me to own an emotion I don't have."

The whole conversation descends into an argument where she accuses me of attacking her.

"You're so smart and so clever. I can never win. I can't compete with you."

"This isn't about anyone winning or losing. It's just about exploring ourselves." She does the "You make me feel inadequate" thing. I ask her what she wants. She says she wants me to be supportive no matter what she says or does.

"You want to be able to express all your feelings to me no matter what they are, but I can only say positive things to you. So there are different rules for you and me, right?"

"That just feels like a mind fuck to me." The conversation lasts at least two hours. She wants to hang up a couple of times. I won't let her. I make us stay on the phone until we have some kind of mutual understanding. I tell her I want her to speak up in the moment rather than save up her grievances and then send me a list of resentments in the mail. I want to deal with each situation as it comes up. She agrees to that.

We finally hang up, but the whole thing still bothers me. Now I can see why she's sick. Her cancer is caused by the anger she nurtures against people who clearly love her. No matter how much I love her, she's constantly angry because I don't love her perfectly enough. She takes the most negative possible interpretation of every interaction and hangs on to it. She's so critical of herself that she only hears criticism coming from other people.

I also feel like she's manipulating me into focusing my attention on her negative game. I write her a letter about all this, but I don't mail it. I know she'll misinterpret everything, and it will just make things worse. I decide it's better not to throw any more energy at it.

At the same time, I take her comments about me to heart. I realize that maybe I am judgmental and critical, but I'm just not conscious of it. If I am relating to people in such a negative way, I should work on changing it. I worry that my New York roommates found me hard to live with but never confronted me about it. I call the production coordinator and tell her about Phoebe's letter.

"I just want to apologize if I came across as judgmental or critical of you. I certainly have no criticisms of you and would never want to make you feel inadequate."

"Honestly, Marsha, I didn't experience you that way at all. In fact, you were the most supportive roommate I ever had. It really helped to be able to bounce things off you."

I debate whether I should spend New Year's with Phoebe as we planned. I decide that I'm a coward if I don't. After all, I'm the one who wants to deal with each complaint as it comes up. Besides, I've been invited to an intriguing New Year's Eve party in New Mexico.

## CHAPTER 15

# WINTER'S CHILL

My friend and fellow film production professional, Catherine Wanek, got fed up with the dark underbelly of Hollywood. She bought an old hunting lodge in a ghost town in southern New Mexico and opened a bed and breakfast. Every year she threw a New Year's Eve bash for the locals. Word of the rockin' party spread wider each year, and each year, the party got bigger. By now, it's a legendary extravaganza. I have a standing invitation. This year, I'm determined to go. The ghost town is not far from Carlsbad Caverns. I've never been there. I ask Phoebe if she'd like to go to the party, and then welcome the New Year with a visit to that hidden treasure of Mother Earth. She says she's up for it.

I fly to Albuquerque the day after Christmas. Phoebe picks me up at the airport. Her hair is short and curly. She looks healthy and slim...almost too slim. We make small talk in the car. I tell her she looks great. I ask about her energy and her diet. She says the nutritionist has adjusted the diet, but what she can eat is still severely limited. I pick my topics carefully. Our relationship feels strained. I search for a comfort zone.

When we get to Phoebe's house, we exchange Christmas gifts. I give her a hand-carved soapstone figure of Kwan-Yin from China for her altar. She gives me a two-volume set of traditional Tibetan healing texts. They're elegant books. It's clearly an expensive gift. Although our adventure together has been about healing, somehow the gift seems impersonal. I thank her for the beautiful gift. She thanks me for everything I've done to help her in the last year. Her speech sounds rehearsed. I suspect that she wrote it out and memorized it. Her delivery has finality to it...like she's making a formal statement that officially fulfills any obligation she feels toward me. I change the subject to cross country skiing.

The next day, we rent skis. Since we don't know a thing about cross country skiing, we ask the young men who work at the sporting goods store to help us figure out what we need. One cute blonde boy flirts with Phoebe. She doesn't seem to notice. I mention it to her when we get back in the car. She dismisses his attention with, "He's too young, and he's probably a jerk."

The next morning, we drive up into the mountains. The pavement is icy. The scenery is breathtaking. The road winds through a pristine blanket of snow. Feathery evergreens wear soft white cloaks. The sky is crystalline blue. The air is clear with a sharp bite. For a Southern California native like me, looking at this beauty through the car window inspires my soul, but being out in the weather is simply unpleasant.

We meet our instructor at the designated parking area. He's a tall, lean older man. He shows us how to put on the skis. He demonstrates the "kick and glide" technique. We try it. I fall immediately. He uses me to demonstrate the correct way to get back up when you fall. It involves getting on your knees and keeping your skis parallel. I feel clumsy and inept. I try to kick and glide again and actually get up a little speed, but I don't know how to stop so I crash into a snow bank. I practice getting up again. He demonstrates how to stop by turning your skis. I try it. It doesn't work. I crash again. He explains that it didn't work because there's a crust of ice on top of the snow from a recent rain. He says it works much better on powder.

"So how do I stop?"

"Just dig in harder. It'll probably work."

It never works for me. I crash at least a hundred times. I get really good at getting back up. I'm concentrating so hard on trying to stay upright that I don't pay much attention to what's going on with Phoebe. I don't think she's crashing as much as I am. She seems to be taking it much slower and avoiding the risk of falling. I can't tell if she's having fun. I'm not. By now, my jeans are soaking wet from falling in the snow and a cold wind is blowing right through them, freezing them against my skin. My feet are so cold they're numb. The most fun I'm having is on the baby downhill slopes. If I tuck into a crouch I can get some speed up without the effort of kicking and gliding. There's a little thrill in seeing the pine trees flash past and feeling the cold air rush by my face. The problem is that the only way I know how to stop is to fall over...then I have to struggle back up again.

I hate this sport. Phoebe asks me if I had a good time. I say, "I think it would be a fun thing to do if the snow was powdery and it was about 70 degrees and sunny."

As we drive back, Phoebe casually tells me that Carlos had a major heart attack. He's out of the hospital now, and Joaquin is taking care of him at home.

"My God! Have you gone to see him?"

"Not yet."

"Well, this is a great opportunity for you to pay them back for all the help they gave you."

"But I'm still working on my own health. I have to concentrate on that. I don't have time to take care of Carlos."

I don't scold. I don't judge. I don't say anything, but I see that Phoebe's just not able to do what I did for her. She's the one who had to look death directly in the eye. I can't blame her for wanting to run away from "La Muerta" now.

The next morning, every muscle of my body is excruciatingly sore. My knees are not black and blue. They're completely black. Every time I fell and got up again, I mashed my knees. I was too numb with cold to feel any pain at the time. Phoebe is sore too. She opts to spend the day in bed. I borrow her car and take off for a day on my own.

I drive out to Santo Domingo pueblo. It's the Festival of the Three Kings. A new chief is installed, and the tribe is performing traditional dances. Performing is really the wrong word to describe the dancing. Like the Drum Dance, the dance is not a performance for an audience but rather a meditation for the dancers. Each tribe has its own specific chants, costumes, rituals and occasions for dancing. The public may or may not be invited to visit during the dances. If you accept an invitation and expect to be entertained, you'll be bored. If you go to honor their sacred intention, you may have your own spiritual experience. As I arrive, the plaza is crowded with four different groups of dancers in beautiful costumes...feathered headdresses, fox pelts hanging from their belts, evergreen boughs tied to their arms. Drums pound. Singers chant. The dancers shift from one foot to the other with the rhythm. The sun is shining, but it's a cold day. Melted snow has turned the ground to red mud. Ice lingers in the shadows. I lean against an adobe wall to watch the dance and zip up my parka for warmth. The dancers break into two lines that move in opposite directions, then turn and move toward each other. The individual dancers' movements are subtle, steady and mesmerizing. As I watch them, I relax and stop worrying about the tension between Phoebe and me. The drums stop, and the dancers leave the plaza. The man standing next to me tells me they're taking a break. He says one of the Santo Domingo families has invited him to the feast at their house. He asks me if I'd like to join him. I'm delighted by my luck. Only insiders get invited into tribal homes for feasting. I've never been invited before. I accept instantly. He introduces himself as Ray. He has a rugged look with dark hair and an open attitude. We shake hands. I like the confidence of his firm grip. I like that he lets me look into his cool gray eyes. He's a construction worker. His sister is a dealer of Native American jewelry. The family we're going to visit are silversmiths who sell to her.

We walk across the plaza and down a side street. He knocks on the door of an adobe house that looks exactly like every other adobe house in the pueblo. A Santo Domingo woman answers the door. We step in and are introduced to about four generations of family: an old grandfather with all his silver and turquoise jewelry, welcoming women, beefy young men in rock 'n roll t-shirts and toddlers scurrying underfoot. I can't remember their names, but it's not awkward because there's not much conversation. I know from being around Joseph and his brothers that silence is considered a polite way to honor other people. If you chatter, it shows that you are not "listening" to the depth of others. I'm surprised at how big the house is. We are greeted in a large living room. A long, bountiful table is set in the adjoining dining room. There's a separate kitchen, and I see doors leading to three or more bedrooms and workshops. The walls of the living room are covered with bright trade blankets and heavy hand woven blankets draped side by side. Blankets are often given as gifts of appreciation or badges of honor. This richly textured rainbow indicates that we're visiting a successful, respected family. We are invited to sit at the table. Bowls of food are passed. We serve ourselves tacos, yams, rice, home-baked bread, hearty beef stew. I especially enjoy the pozole, spicy chili soup with hominy. I compliment the food and praise the women's culinary skills. They seem pleased. I tentatively try to ask a question about the symbolism behind the dance. I get a terse answer from the elder man. I drop the subject. Clearly, it's not something that can be explained to a naïve white woman. There's no hostility in the exchange. It doesn't change the warmth of the family's hospitality. After we eat, we express our gratitude and go back out to the plaza to watch some more dancing. One group is a comic act...in black face with white beards and wigs and flowers in their hair. I can't understand a word of the dialogue, but I can tell by the crowd's reaction that they are really funny. The dancers are intensely concentrated...in deep meditation to the beat of the drum. The spectators are still and reverent (except during the funny parts) wrapped in their bright striped blankets. As the shadows get long, the temperature drops even lower. I thank Ray and say I'm going to head back to Albuquerque.

"Have you ever been to Midnight Rodeo?"

"What's that?"

"It's a country western dance hall. Would you like to go?"

"I've never been country and western dancing. I don't know how to do it."

"Then I'll teach you. It's easy."

"Sounds fun."

## CHAPTER 16

# AWAKENING THE NEW

The next morning, I rent a car and take off. I drive south. It feels good to be alone in the vast desert. It's a relief to be free of Phoebe's dark moods and control games. I stop and buy Mexican-grown watermelons to contribute to the potluck. It'll be fun to eat summer picnic food in the dead of winter. I continue south. At Truth or Consequences, I get off the highway and head west on a two-lane road. The terrain changes to wooded hills. Patches of snow peek out from between the trees. After four hours of driving, I arrive at Catherine's lodge.

A wagon wheel leans against the fence. Tall pines tower over the rough stone structure. Cars are parked everywhere already. I go inside and ask for Catherine. I'm told she's upstairs. We meet on the staircase and hug. She asks where my friend is. I tell her she's not coming. Catherine shows me to my bed. It's a bunk in a room set up as a women's dorm for the New Year's festivities. She takes me on a tour of the lodge. It's three stories with an attached greenhouse and various outbuildings. It's in a gorgeous setting, nestled against the edge of the Gila National Wilderness. I carry my watermelons into the communal kitchen and join other party guests in preparing food and setting up expansive buffet tables. More people arrive. The buffet tables fill with salads, chili, enchiladas, lasagna, bread pudding, carrot cake, brownies and countless other temptations. The invitation says the soiree is a formal occasion, so just before party time, the women change into thrift store ball gowns and the men put on tuxedo-print T-shirts or top hats and blue jeans.

By nine o'clock, the place is packed. Soggy paper plates overflow the trash cans. The buffet tables have been ravaged, but new food is being added all the time. There's live music by a parade of folk singers, bluegrass bands and Celtic groups. The guests are a truly eclectic lot: children and old folks, singles and couples, Hispanics and Anglos, ranchers and artists, old hippies and desert rats, small town characters and even a Hollywood movie star who appeared in a movie shot on location near here. Since people have to bring their own booze, there's not that much drinking. A few people go outside to smoke joints in the icy night air.

I go to the bathroom. Several women are waiting in line. I introduce myself to them, and one of them immediately brings up her incest issues. The others join in right away. Sexual abuse seems to be the topic of the moment. Suddenly, women everywhere are discussing it openly,

After my turn in the toilet, I wander back to the kitchen and strike up a conversation with an arty-elegant woman of a certain age. Her silver blonde hair is pulled back into a sleek bun. She looks a little out of place among the pony-tailed cowboys and earthy young goddesses. I comment on her hand-crafted silver earrings. She says she made them herself. She speaks with a Scandinavian accent. I ask her where she's from. She was born in Denmark but now lives in Ohio. She's here visiting her son who built his own adobe house nearby. She tells me her son has a degree in linguistics and speaks five languages. He's traveled extensively, is very interested in ecological issues and may join the Peace

Corps.

"Your son sounds like a fascinating person."

"He is. I'll introduce you to him...as soon as he finishes playing."

"He's a musician too?"

"Yes. He's the one playing piano right now."

I study the tall, blonde man accompanying the Celtic musicians. For some reason, he looks vaguely familiar.

After he basks in applause, his mother introduces us. His name is Sam. He's about 20 years younger than I am. I'm just a little younger than his mother. We talk about our world travels. While I've been all over Asia, he's backpacked around South America and lived in Uruguay. He's spent a lot of time in Turkey and has even picked up some of the language. He's good at languages, maybe because he learned Danish as a child while visiting his mother's family. He also speaks Swedish and is fluent in Spanish.

We continue to talk as we serve ourselves from the buffet. We retire to a corner table to eat and lose ourselves in conversation. He tells me about the house he designed and built and how he made every adobe brick by hand. The house is round with bottle windows. It has electricity from solar panels on the roof and solar-heated water. He also designed a low tech composting toilet because he feels flushing is an outrageous waste of water. He spent two years on the project. Now it's finished, and he's looking for his next challenge.

He listens as I talk about my career, my spiritual work with Joseph and my involvement in Phoebe's healing. He's skeptical about Joseph. His previous girlfriend got involved with some Middle Eastern cult, so he's wary of gurus and people who follow them without question. I assure him that Joseph's not on a power trip, and I do question him all the time. I told him how my husband was convinced I'd joined a cult when he flipped out during the Buddhist meditation retreat. A new band starts to play 60s rock 'n roll. He asks me if I want to dance. I do. We find our way to the dance floor. As we move to the beat, I study the intelligent eyes behind his round wire-rimmed glasses, his full expressive lips, his soft pale hair, his tall lanky frame. I realize that he looks familiar because I dreamed him. I saw this face, this body, this man in my dream about the two sisters. Sam is the doctor who rents a room in the whorehouse with the dark sister. I realize that in some way, probably a sexual way, he will help me heal myself. The music changes to a slow dance. We hold each other. I press my body against his. If he's noticed our age difference, he doesn't seem to care.

Midnight comes. The party guests break into wild cheers. We kiss. He asks if I want to go outside and get some fresh air.

The cold air is shocking. He gets a blanket out of his car, and we cuddle up under it on a swing hanging from a big pine tree. I tell him that I dreamed him. I tell him the dream...except for the last scene in the whorehouse.

"But I'm not a doctor."

"Maybe you're going to get a Ph.D."

"I've thought about it."

"Or maybe you'll heal me in some way."

When I tell him the part of the dream where my ex-husband pounds a nail through the painting of me, he asks, "What part of your body did the nail go through?" The same question Joseph asked.

I tell him about listening to the women openly discussing incest while waiting to use the rest room.

I say, "It's good that so many women are speaking out and getting help, but I worry about the men who are the perpetrators. They never admit it, much less get help. It's a dark, cancerous time bomb growing in many men."

He says, "You know it isn't only women who are the victims. Men can be the victims too." Then he tells me the story of how he was molested by an older gay man friend when he was a young teenager. His story gives me a completely new perspective on the subject and shifts me away from thinking of sexual abuse as a crime against women by men. I wonder if this is the healing. Maybe it's already complete. We hold each other under the blanket.

It gets too cold, so we go inside. Some musicians invite Sam to play with them. We go in a back room. I listen while they play lively Irish folk music. Sam plays mandolin and guitar and tin whistle.

He asks me what I'm doing tomorrow. I tell him I'm meeting Phoebe at Carlsbad Caverns.

I ask him, "Have you ever been there?"

"No. I haven't."

"Do you want to go?"

"As a matter of fact, I do." I wonder if Phoebe will be offended if I bring him along. She shouldn't be. After all, she broke her New Year's date with me. I decide to indulge in something pleasurable for me. Sam and I make plans to meet there. He has to take his parents to the airport in El Paso tomorrow.

At four in the morning, we decide we need some sleep. I sleep in my bunk bed in the women's dorm. He sleeps on the floor of a room where his parents share a bed. My sleep is restless, and I get up about eight. He and his mother are in the kitchen washing the dishes from the night before. The party is still going on.

We have coffee and orange juice. He has to take his parents to El Paso airport. We agree to take the long way to Carlsbad through El Paso and look for each other on the road. They take off for the airport. I hike into the forest with Catherine. We do a little ceremony and offer some prayers of intention for the New Year.

I thank Catherine and drive about four or five hours through drizzle, through desert, through fog, through Texas to Carlsbad. I look for his car the whole way. I wonder if I should speed up to catch up with him or slow down to let him catch up with me. I arrive at the motel just after sundown. He's pulled into the parking lot about a minute before me.

He says, "I was wondering the whole way if you were ahead of me or behind me. I didn't stop because I was afraid I'd fall further behind you...but if I would have, we probably would have found each other."

We laugh and go into the lobby. Phoebe hasn't checked in yet. I leave a note for her, and we go to eat in the motel restaurant.

I ask him if he wants to get a single room for himself or if he would like to share a room with me. I say either arrangement is alright with me. He says it isn't easy for him to be sexual with a woman until he knows her well. We talk about the pros and cons of being friends versus being friends and lovers. I point out that our age difference means that a relationship as lovers would probably be temporary. We talk about how a non-monogamous relationship might make sense for people who live in different states and travel a lot. We don't disagree on anything.

Finally he says, "It would be nice to get a room together." I suggest we split the cost. He agrees. Phoebe arrives on cue. I introduce her to Sam and ask her if she would like to have a room to herself. She says she would.

Sam and I move in like two travelers sharing a room. I unpack a few things. He fools with the thermostat. He takes a shower with the door closed and comes out wrapped in a towel. I take a shower with the door closed and come out in my sweatsuit. He's in one of the two beds. I crawl in beside him. We cuddle and kiss. He says he wants to watch a little TV for fun. There's nothing good on. We snap it off and kiss and caress. My sweatsuit comes off. The lights go out. We enjoy each other's bodies. We touch and kiss and caress sensuously. I'm so aroused by his touch that energy starts to pump from my solar plexus out my extremities. My hands are so full of chi that they start to spasm and become paralyzed. It's similar to what I experienced during breathwork. My kundalini kicks into overdrive. Sexual encounters interrupt our sleep.

In the morning, we take a hot bath together and go to breakfast. I tell him I would love to see his adobe house. He invites me to visit him when we leave Carlsbad. I accept the invitation. When Phoebe comes to breakfast, I tell her I'm going to go to Sam's instead of going back to Albuquerque with her.

The Caverns are an otherworldly adventure. Phoebe hurries ahead of us. As we descend into a gaping hole and go underground, I think about my wild west dream. The dark sister and the doctor rent a basement room in the whorehouse. Sam and I wander in a trance through the mysterious womb of mother earth. In this basement of the planet, I feel like I'm in an altered state, hypnotized by magical stone spirits. The silence is so deep that we don't want to speak. We point and whisper when we see watchful faces or ancient deities frozen in the rock. We're enchanted by the fancifully decorated ballrooms of fairy royalty.

When we finally emerge into the light, it's after noon. We eat lunch with Phoebe and study the map to plot our route back to Sam's territory. Phoebe heads for Albuquerque. We drive back through Texas, and this time, it's sunny. We weave our way through El Paso, eat Mexican food in Mesilla, get gas and groceries in Demming. It's night by the time we get to the tiny bordertown where he lives.

His house takes my breath away. It reminds me of a kiva. Even in the dark, I can see its earthy beauty. Inside, it's a cozy mud nest. I know I can curl up and be comfortable here. He builds a fire in the wood stove in the middle of the round room and makes tea. He shows me how to use the composting toilet he's devised. It's a bucket of sawdust set in the floor. You squat over it, then shovel more sawdust in. When it's full he takes it outside and buries the sawdust. He's right; it doesn't smell. We drink tea and talk for a while. I tell him I need to sleep. We go to bed and fall asleep in each other's arms. We make love in the morning.

Finally he says, "You know, we've been in this bed for 10 hours."

I say, "Good." We get up and eat granola and bananas.

We venture outside the house. It's even more beautiful in daylight. The blue-green bottles set in the walls cast colored light inside. He's used tires as eaves around the earthen roof and set Mexican tiles into the walls. He painted "adobegylphs" of primitive animals and mythological figures on the exterior. There are Chinese characters painted on a tile on the door. I ask him if he knows what they mean.

"Yes, I copied them out of a book. It says 'Mud Palace.'"

He takes me on a walking tour of the intentional community where he lives. The desert is scattered with excavations. Old hippies and young visionaries are building houses out of old tires and beer cans, cement domes, adobe bricks and pyramids. We meet a neighbor who is a pagan goddess-worshipper. His house is a hobbit hole. He made a breast-shaped mound of earth, covered it with reinforced concrete, then dug out the earth. His round pit-house is warm, dark and cozy…a great place to hibernate. His van is covered with tree bark. He spends his days making earth sculptures of the Goddess, covering the roof of his house with mosaics of stone and creating organic-looking silver jewelry.

Sam shows me the community center. It boasts a library, full kitchen, flush toilet, shower, laundry, telephone, TV, VCR and ping pong table. I phone Phoebe to be sure she got home safely. I tell her I'm going to stay another night. We go into town to replenish his supply of drinking water.

Columbus, New Mexico, consists of a post office, gas station, library, bar, three restaurants, gallery and gift shop. He gets water from a vending machine outside one of the restaurants. We visit his friends who run the gallery. He plays their upright piano as I buy ceramics with Mimbres designs. The gallery comes alive with his music. As I watch him play, my heart opens. I want to be with him.

That night we cross the border to have dinner in Mexico. We park on the American side and walk across. We go to a large empty restaurant. We're the only patrons, but the Mariachis start to play when we arrive and continue to serenade us through dinner. We dance...the only couple on the huge dance floor. The food is great. The people are friendly. The streets are cold and muddy. As we walk back into America, the border guard on duty recognizes Sam.

"Hi, Sam. How are you? Is this your mother?"

"No. This is my friend, Marsha." We laugh and shake hands. I'm embarrassed. I laugh as we walk to the car.

"I guess I better get used to that."

"Yeah, just call me Eddy Rex." He proceeds to make a whole series of Oedipus jokes. He wins my heart with his poise, deft humor and sincere self-assurance. I really like this guy.

We go to bed and make love. The sun rises and all I want is to give him pleasure. We make love again and doze in the afterglow.

We go take a shower. It's late in the morning, and there's only cold water. I squeal and quickly splash myself clean. We eat lunch at the community center with the other residents. We go back to Mud Palace. I pack my bag. He produces a map of Los Angeles and asks me to show him where I live. He tells me he plans to visit L.A. on his way to Argentina in early February. I invite him to stay with me. He accepts my invitation. We both agree that our affection for each other does not imply an agreement of monogamy.

He suggests we take a walk in the desert. We stroll up an arroyo. I'm comfortable in his company and feel a little sad about parting.

We walk back to the house. I load my bag into the car. He says he has to mail a letter and asks me to drop him off at the post office in Columbus. We drive into town and kiss goodbye in the car. I drive away. As I drive to Albuquerque, I wonder if I'll see him again.

CHAPTER 17

# ENDING THE OLD

Phoebe doesn't have much to say when I get back. I can tell she's mad, but she won't admit it. She ignores me. Finally, I break the tense silence between us.

"Are you jealous?"

"Of course not! What a stupid question."

"Then what are you feeling?"

"I'm feeling like I don't want to see you any more."

"What?"

"Listen, I really appreciate everything you did for me, but I don't want to continue the friendship."

"Why?"

"Because I never really liked you in the first place."

"We've been friends for thirty years, and you never liked me?"

"That's right. We always only did the things you wanted to do."

"Excuse me! Planting your garden, painting your fence, throwing your birthday party, going fucking cross country skiing? The only thing I said I wanted to do this entire year was go to the New Year's Eve party, and you didn't even do that!"

"This year wasn't typical."

Could it be true that she didn't like me when we were in college listening to Bob Dylan and the Rolling Stones, when we protested the Vietnam War and spoke out for feminism? She didn't like me when she came and stayed with me when she needed to get away from her husband? She didn't like me when we went on twilight hikes in the magnificent desert outside Tucson? She didn't like me when she showed me around her beloved island of Oahu? She didn't like me when she called and asked me to help her move from Tucson to Albuquerque? She didn't like me when we made a pact to take care of each other in case of serious illness? She didn't like me when I spent all night sitting in a chair in her hospital room because she was afraid to be alone?

Did I spend thirty years forcing my friendship on a person who didn't want it? Or is Phoebe just a skillful user?

"Well, you sure knew who to call when you were in trouble, didn't you?"

I pack my bags and move to Marsha Mason's luxury ranch. I planned to visit her anyway, so I'm just showing up a couple of days early. I've finished rewriting the screenplay. I hand her a copy of the new draft. She's excited to get it and promises to read it right away. I tell her about the New Year's Eve party, my fling with Sam and the rift with Phoebe. Marsha says she thinks Phoebe is afraid that she'll never be able to return the huge favor I've done for her and wants out of the obligation. It could be true. Phoebe certainly balked at the idea of repaying the kindness of Carlos and Joaquin.

"You know, not everyone has the strength to do what you did."

"She could say that. She doesn't need make up some bogus excuse to end a thirty-year friendship."

"She can't admit it to herself. What do you want?"

"I'd like to continue the friendship but in a more balanced way. We need to get back to being peers."

"You're the leader and the teacher?"

"Now…yes."

"So you need to let her take the lead. Anything you figure out or do to correct the situation will confirm that you're the powerful one."

"So she has to fix it."

"Yes. All you can do is to be vulnerable."

I spend the next day being alternately angry and sad. I feel used. I have conversations inside my head. "I'm such a fool. Am I blind...or just stupid...or both? She's been in my life longer than any lover, and now she just wants to end it without even trying to work it out. I can't let that happen."

I look down at my hand. I see my little finger...polarity. Phoebe and I are in polarity. I see my ring finger...reconciliation. That's what's next.

I call Joseph. We come up with an idea for a joint counseling session where he'll mediate while Phoebe and I speak our differences. It's worth a try. At least, it's a situation that puts us on equal footing. I'm not sure Phoebe will go for it. I call her.

"Listen, I'm not willing to blow off thirty years of friendship without at least trying to work things out."

"I don't think it's going to do any good to talk about it."

"What if we had a mediator? You know, someone impartial who could referee."

"Like who?"

"I'm willing to go with anyone you suggest, but if you don't know someone, Joseph's willing to do it."

I listen to silence on the other end of the phone. Finally, Phoebe speaks.

"OK. When?"

"Tomorrow. Two o'clock. Joseph's place."

"OK." Phoebe hangs up.

Phoebe's never been to Joseph's. She's never been in a sweatlodge. She never got around to making three hundred tobacco bundles. I've never asked her to reimburse me for the money I paid Joseph to come to the hospital. I realize I've done a lot more to heal her than she's done to heal herself.

## CHAPTER 18

# OUR ONLY ENEMY

Joseph and I sit in his kiva and wait for Phoebe. We're both uncomfortable. I feel like he wishes he hadn't agreed to mediate. I just feel like a failure. I was trying to help a friend in trouble, and now she hates me. I must have screwed up somewhere for things to go so wrong. Then again, things haven't gone completely wrong. Phoebe's alive and cancer-free. What if I hadn't helped her? Would she be alive or dead today? There's no way to know.

Joseph asks why Phoebe's approval is important to me.

"Because I care about her. Our friendship is the longest relationship I've ever had. She's more like a sister than my sisters."

He nods and doesn't pursue the question any further.

Phoebe finally shows up. We greet each other. Joseph asks her about her health. She says she's feeling much better.

"And how are you feeling about Marsha?"

With no further prompting, Phoebe starts reciting a laundry list of things she doesn't like about me. I make her feel inadequate by always acting competent. I make her feel stupid by being a know-it-all. I don't let her have her true feelings by always trying to get her to look on the bright side. I make her life seem boring by talking about how interesting my life is. I've always got some suggestion about what she should be doing instead of praising her for what she is doing. When I'm around, her friends are more interested in me than they are in her. I'm critical of everything she does. I'm always trying to "fix" her which is not what she wants from a friend.

When she finally pauses for breath, I say "All that may be true. I'm not denying that I'm critical, but I'm not keeping a list of everything I don't like about you."

"You see what I mean?" she snaps at Joseph. "She's always got some smart comeback to put me down."

Joseph asks me what I'm feeling.

"I'm not keeping a list about what I don't like about Phoebe, because I like everything about Phoebe. She's always complaining about how unhappy she is, so I try to suggest ways for her to be happy." Phoebe interrupts me.

"See, there's another criticism. Remember when I asked you if you thought I should move away from Tucson, and you said, 'Why not? You've done nothing but complain about everybody there?' That really hurt me. It was a mean thing to say."

"But you did nothing but complain about everybody the whole time you lived there."

"See what I mean?"

Joseph gently whispers to Phoebe to let me finish.

"I hear Phoebe saying that she wants to be able to say whatever she's feeling…which is fine with me. The problem is she has lots of rules about what I can and cannot say if I want to be her friend. It feels like a one-way street."

Joseph turns to Phoebe. In the softest, most neutral voice, he asks, "Phoebe, if Marsha can accept you the way you are, can you accept her the way she is?" Phoebe answers without the slightest hesitation, "No."

"Marsha, are you willing to change so Phoebe can love you?"

"No. I want to be loved and accepted for who I am too."

"Then I think Phoebe's right. I think you should end the friendship."

The shock of his words takes my breath away. Phoebe smirks with satisfaction.

"This was a good idea, Marsha. I'm glad you suggested it."

Tears stream down my cheeks. Phoebe shows no emotion at all. Joseph asks me if I'm angry.

"I think I'm more sad."

"Answer yes or no. Are you angry?"

"Yes."

"Why?

"I guess I feel unappreciated."

"It's important to express that or you'll feel resentful."

Phoebe asks if I'd like to get a letter from her telling me what she appreciates about me.

"Yes...but I think the whole idea of letters is dumb. I'd rather tell you in person what I appreciate about you."

"That's not how I operate. I'd be much more comfortable with a letter."

Joseph asks Phoebe if she'd like a response from me to her letter.

"If she feels like it. I don't want to invalidate Marsha's feelings of being unappreciated."

I sit in numb silence as she writes Joseph a check for half the cost of the session, closes her purse, hefts it onto her shoulder, walks out the door and closes it behind her. She doesn't want to invalidate my feelings of being unappreciated? Is that because I'm not appreciated? Or I'm entitled to my feelings even if they are inaccurate? Talk about a mind-fuck...

"Joseph?"

"You have to let her go. You can't save her."

"She's so full of anger, I'm scared for her."

"That's why she's sick. Her lack of gratitude is killing her. We heal ourselves by giving thanks every day for our life, for our breath, for the beauty around us, for the people who love us. It's much healthier for you to release her. I've had those people in my life who can't tell me how they feel to my face but want to write me letters all the time. Believe me, you're much better off when they're gone."

"Why couldn't I heal her?"

"Because we can't heal other people, Marsha. We can only heal ourselves."

"But you healed me."

"No. You healed yourself. Sometimes we can help other people learn to heal themselves…if they ask to be healed, if they want to be healed, if they are willing to do the work of healing. She says she doesn't want you to fix her. It's a lie. She wants someone to give her a magic bullet that will make this all go away. You're showing her resources that she can use to heal herself. That's what makes her mad. She doesn't want to do the work. I showed you what to do. You did the work. Phoebe didn't. Even more important, you take responsibility for your life. Phoebe doesn't take responsibility for anything."

"What do you mean?"

"Phoebe wants to blame everybody else for making her unhappy. Did you hear everything she blamed you for? It's not your fault she feels inadequate. She feels inadequate. That's her stuff. Remember this, Marsha. Never, ever blame anyone else for what happens to you."

"But sometimes people do bad things to you...like rob your house...or tell you they never liked you after you spent a year nursing them through a serious illness."

"You agreed to it."

"I agreed to let somebody rob my house?"

"There's something you want to learn from it. Before we come here, when we're in the place between worlds, we review what we've learned in our past lives and we decide what we want to learn in our next life. Then we agree to all these experiences that will teach us that thing we want to learn. When we're born, we forget our agreement. We spend our whole lives trying to remember it."

"I don't know if I believe that."

"You don't have to literally believe it. Just live your life as if you do. When you blame others, you give your power away to them. Phoebe kept giving her power to you and then resenting you for taking it."

"So give me an example of learning from a bad experience."

"Remember when you had that accident when you got rear-ended?"

"Yeah."

"You said you thought it was a spiritual event."

"Yeah. It seemed like more than just an accident, but I still don't understand why."

"Imagine yourself back there. Imagine yourself watching yourself during the accident."

I close my eyes. I hover above my Toyota and watch myself negotiate stop and go traffic as I make the transition from the

Harbor Freeway southbound to the Santa Monica Freeway westbound. I'm going to a business luncheon, so I'm nicely dressed in a jacket and skirt with silver and malachite earrings. I see an old blue Ford behind me. The driver's not paying attention. I brake for the car in front of me. He doesn't brake and slams into my trunk. We're not going fast, but the impact jerks my head back so hard that my earrings fly off. The back of my head connects with the headrest with a whack! I see something shatter inside me. Some crystallized pattern crumbles into thousands of little pie-shaped pieces. At the same instant, my knee connects with the dashboard. It's the same knee that my husband drove the nail through in the dream.

"Something shattered inside me."

"What was it?"

"Something crystallized. A pattern."

"An old behavior pattern."

"And the nail went through my knee."

"Completion. You finished with that pattern and agreed to let it be broken to bits. You're a warrior, Marsha."

"Me?"

"Yes. You're not afraid to change. You're not afraid to look at your own darkness. You're not afraid to do battle with mankind's only enemy."

"What's our only enemy?"

"Our fear that we're not loveable. That's what Phoebe is really afraid to look at. That's what makes everybody do what they do. All the other issues boil down to that one issue. We all have the same primal wound."

"Did I want to heal Phoebe so she'd love me?"

"Did you?"

"I guess so."

"And you feel powerful when you're the healer."

"Yeah…"

"And you feel superior to the person you're trying to heal?"

"And if I took care of her, she'd be there to take care of me if I needed help."

"Or maybe you just loved her. It's complicated. You're a warrior because you're brave enough to take an honest look at all of it."

"What if I see that I am unlovable?"

"The challenge is to learn to love ourselves in all of our imperfection."

"You mean I'm not perfect?"

"Phoebe's not wrong about you making her feel disempowered. She gave you her power, but you were willing to take it."

"What should I have done?"

"You could have let her do more for herself and waited for her to ask for help."

"Sometimes she did."

"And sometimes she didn't. You were probably in a no-win situation anyway. I think she invites people to rescue her and then gets mad at them when they try. You try to heal her, and it confirms her false belief that someone else can fix her, so she gets mad at you for not being successful. You step into a trap she sets where everything is your fault. One of your imperfections is your willingness to give more help than is helpful. I think it's a beautiful flaw."

"Thanks. I think…"

"Here's another thing to remember. A warrior never complains. When you don't like something, change it or accept it. Don't waste energy complaining about it."

"But that's what I was trying to get Phoebe to do. She said I wouldn't let her express her feelings."

"There's a big difference between complaining and expressing feelings. The ultimate result of the sweatlodges and the dances and all the work we do is that you become like a hollow bone. Emotions flow through you. You feel everything...anger, sadness, joy. You feel and express all your emotions, but you don't attach to them. You aren't your feelings. You're the bone. You're always ready to let new feelings pass through you without judging them. Emotions aren't good or bad. Different emotions weave together in the fabric of life. Complaining is focusing on negativity and blaming someone or something else for it. Focusing on negativity draws more negativity to you."

"So why didn't you tell Phoebe this?"

"Phoebe's not a warrior. She's not ready to hear any of it."

"Will she be all right?"

"I don't know, Marsha. Don't try to contact her again."

I fight back tears as I write a check for my half of the cost of the session.

That night Ray takes me to Midnight Rodeo. The place is huge. It has several bars, and the dance floor is like a racetrack with a bar in the middle. It's packed with people in cowboy boots. I'm the only one in tennis shoes. The dancers all move around the floor in the same direction like cars on a circular freeway. Ray teaches me to do the Texas Two-Step (it's not too complicated...step together, walk, walk), Texas Swing (I can fake that one). I even pick up

Cotton-Eyed Joe. It's not my favorite kind of music, but it's fun anyway. I feel like I'm getting an inside look at another culture. We each have one beer. He takes me back to Marsha Mason's house. When he kisses me goodnight on her front porch, I recognize him. He's the dark man that the blond sister chooses in my wild west dream.

## CHAPTER 19

# SUN MOON DANCE

I go back to my grueling life as a cog in the show business machine. Marsha Mason loves the rewrite and sends it off to her A-list Hollywood agent. Something has shifted in me. The life of ceremony seems so much more vital than entertainment industry wheeling and dealing. The intensity and excitement of working on a movie set now pales in comparison to the risk and drama of my inner explorations.

I feel unfulfilled in my career and often slip into sadness. My work with Joseph has changed me...in a good way, but as I grow, I leave people that I love behind. My bond with Phoebe and my bond with Jack both began in the sixties. We all saw ourselves as victims of "the establishment." We protested against "the man". We struggled to express our anger at a system that we felt oppressed us...and maybe it actually did. Somewhere along the way, I decided to choose happiness...even though the world wasn't perfect. Jack and Phoebe chose to stay stuck in being angry victims. Maybe they saw me as a traitor. Maybe I am. I love their anger. It's righteous. It can motivate change. Right or wrong, they stay in that place of polarity while I move through reconciliation, unity, purpose and, hopefully, transformation of potential. For me, there's no turning back. I embrace my new life as it unfolds. At the same time, leaving old friends behind makes me sad. I watch the mail for a letter from Phoebe. Months pass, and I give up hope. I get funny, sweet letters from Sam. His Argentina trip gets postponed indefinitely along with his plans to visit me in L.A. Ray calls occasionally to ask when I'm coming back to New Mexico.

Joseph suggests that I come in July for the Sun Moon Dance. I jump at the chance. The Sun Moon Dance is one of Joseph's non-traditional versions of the "dance fast" which is practiced in different variations by many Native American tribes. The Ghost Dance movement of the 1800s is a historic example of focused group trance dancing. The ecstatic empowerment cultivated by the fasting dancers, who often danced until they collapsed in deep trance, was so powerful that it frightened their oppressors into a violent reaction resulting in the tragic massacre of unarmed men, women and children at Wounded Knee in 1890. For many years, the dances and all Native American spiritual rituals were banned by the Bureau of Indian Affairs. Thankfully, wise ancestors secretly kept the ceremonies alive.

Joseph's tribe, the Southern Utes, practice a Sun Dance where men dance in a corral with a forked tree trunk in the center for four days with no food or water. Warriors inspired by spirit "hit the tree", that is they run and purposely collide with the tree trunk. They're often knocked down. Sometimes, they're knocked unconscious. Once a dancer hits the tree, he's taken out of the dance. As a young man, Joseph broke both front teeth when he hit the tree. Since Joseph doesn't strictly adhere to Native traditions, he allows women to participate in the dance. He recognized that including feminine energy creates a healing balance for the earth and her people. That's why he calls it the Sun Moon Dance.

The advance instructions for the Sun Moon Dance are pretty similar to the Drum Dance except we're supposed to bring four white sheets and two small towels. We're also invited to bring a support person with us to care for our personal needs during the dance. I'd like to have a support person, but who? I have no husband or grown children. My sisters disapprove of me "playing Indian." I consider asking Sam or Ray, but in a moment of vanity, I decide I don't want either one of them to see me after four days without a shower. All my women friends have demanding jobs or children to care for. The main thing I'm worried about is being too spaced out to drive back to Albuquerque safely after the dance. I decide if that's a problem, I'll stay and camp at the dance site until I'm grounded enough to drive. I'll dance alone.

I'm looking forward to four days of dancing. After Drum Dance, I feel like I can handle a four-day dry fast. I have my doubts about hitting the tree...or more accurately, I don't understand the rationale behind hitting the tree. Or maybe, I just don't want to hit the tree. At least, I want to talk to Joseph about it before the dance begins.

I'm apprehensive and emotional as my plane takes off for New Mexico. I have a premonition of myself in the hospital. I'm afraid. I'm afraid that my will to endure four days is stronger than my good sense. I'm afraid that my ego will drive me to accomplish the goal, and in the process, I won't allow myself to be vulnerable enough to receive the teachings. The plane lifts off, flies over Santa Monica beach and heads out over the vast blue of the Pacific Ocean. As we make the turn to go east, I look down and see a school of dolphins playing in the sea directly beneath us. I laugh at myself and relax into the journey.

I get to Joseph's just in time for the sweatlodge. After the first round, I have a strong intuition that I shouldn't stay in for the next round. It's a bewildering feeling. By now, I've done many sweatlodges. I've never left a lodge while it was in progress. I know there's no danger. What I'm feeling is not fear or discomfort. It's as though I'm hearing a clear voice telling me that it's dangerous for me to stay in the lodge. I ignore the voice. When the door closes for the second round, I start to cry. As soon as the steam comes up, I convulse into violent dry heaves.

"Joseph, please let me out!" He tells the firekeeper to open the door, and I crawl out. I lie on the earth next to the fire during the second and third rounds. The nausea leaves me. The voice tells me the danger has passed. I go back into the lodge for the fourth round. I pray that I will have the strength to dance and also have the openness to truly absorb the lessons.

I lie awake most of the night, but when I do sleep, I dream about my father. I'm helping him clean out his den, trying to get him to throw old stuff away. He isn't willing to let go of very much including a cheap cigar, an old black leather coin purse, a souvenir wastebasket that says "Rocky Point" and has a picture of a Monterey pine. He wants to smoke the cigar and thinks the wastebasket is still good. Is this dream about sex? The phallic symbol and the receptacle? My wounded masculine side burning a tobacco offering in the dreamtime? I tell him to be careful not to burn down the house.

In the morning, I get to Joseph's early so I can talk to him alone.

"Joseph, is it better to hit the tree or to still be dancing at the end of four days?"

"One isn't better than the other. The point is to learn to listen to your true intuition. If you want to stop, ask yourself if you just want to get out of the discomfort or if you've truly learned what you need to learn. Don't hit the tree unless it calls to you."

"How will I know if it's calling to me?"

"You'll know. If you're not sure, it isn't."

"You know, last night I had an intuition that I should leave the lodge after the first round."

"Why didn't you?"

"Ego, I guess. I didn't want to seem like a wimp."

"Good. You learned to recognize intuition. Now pay attention to it and act on it."

I drive up to the dance site with Joseph's brother Tayo. Storm clouds are gathering. He laughs and says, "You're going to get very wet." We arrive at a location in the Sandia Mountains where I've never been before. The corral is a large permanent structure built of two by fours. The tree in the center isn't forked. It's one straight trunk decorated with a buffalo skull, feathers, and dried sage. Cloth streamers in the colors of the four directions flutter from the top. I ask Joseph why it's not forked.

"When we went to cut a new tree for this dance, one of the arms of the fork broke off when it fell. It's a sign that this dance needs a new energy…the single pole."

We set up our tents outside the corral. We'll go into the corral with just our sleeping bags, our dance rattles and our four white sheets. We won't come out for four days…except to go to the outhouse, and when we do that, we must be shrouded in one of our sheets. The sheets can also be hung from the overhead frame around the circumference of the corral to create privacy or shade.

The support team is a tribe unto itself. There must be at least twenty "dog soldiers" and "moon mothers" assisting thirty-five dancers. I tell the head dog soldier that I don't have a support person of my own. He says, "Don't worry. You'll be well supported." Just the idea that someone is going to take care of me makes me cry.

We all work together stretching tarps over the frame around the corral to create an arbor for shade and some protection from the imminent summer rain. Magnificent clouds threaten, but it's sunny and hot. Cicadas are roaring. The heady fragrance of sage and cedar hangs in the crystal blue air. I give offerings of tobacco to Joseph and the drummers. The moon mothers collect the towels we brought.

Joseph calls all the dancers together and reminds us of our agreements. Once we enter the corral, no food or water. We stay in complete silence. We shroud ourselves in a white sheet when we leave the corral to go to the bathroom in order to hold our energy in and create a temporary container for us when we are outside the container of the corral. Joseph says the white sheets help us enter into the white light (which includes all the colors of the rainbow). He tells us not to wear any metal in the corral since it could attract lightning. He announces that this year, dancers won't be taken out and given water after they hit the tree. It seems in past years, some dancers were hitting the tree early just to avoid discomfort.

"Some of you may be tempted to drink water secretly to make it through. If you do that, you only cheat yourself. You'll never know if you could have made it."

He gives each one of us a whistle made from a turkey bone that we are to blow while we dance. These "hollow bones' connect us to the master plan that Great Spirit has for each of us. Blowing our breath through the turkey bone is our constant reminder to be like a hollow bone. It's a turkey bone instead of an eagle bone because the ultimate intention behind this dance is world peace. The turkey is a bird of peace and generosity.

Joseph continues, "I thank you for your sacrifice. You have much to gain from the effort you're about to make. This dance will put you more in touch with supernatural power than any other shamanic technique. Hallucinogenic plants, guided journeys, vision quests...none of them come close to being able to teach you what you will learn from this dance."

Then he sends us to get dressed and tells us to meet at the entrance to the corral in half an hour wearing our turkey bone whistles and wrapped in our white sheets. I go to my tent. As I'm getting dressed, blood starts to pour from my nose. I blot it with tissue and lie down until the bleeding stops. Is this my blood sacrifice?

Half an hour later, I'm part of a clan of ghostly pagan figures. We look more like spirits than humans as the late afternoon breeze flutters our soft white shapes.

We fill our hands with cornmeal, a concrete expression of prosperity, of abundance, of life itself. Following Joseph's lead, we start to blow our turkey bone whistles. Shrill screeching cuts through the low buzz of cicadas and swells to fill the evening air. We walk single file around the outside of the corral. At each of the cardinal points, there's a different shrine. In the east, at the entrance to the corral, a tall phallic stone thrusts out of the earth with small crystals set on either side. In the south, the point of a huge crystal protrudes from the ground. In the north, a cleaved round stone resembles a vagina set in the earth. In the west, a pure white boulder glows in the twilight. Each dancer sprinkles each shrine with cornmeal. With our whistles still screaming, we circle the corral and make offerings at the shrines again...and again...and again. Our chain of pale pilgrims circumscribes the sacred space four times. Once for each point of the compass, for each season, for each element. In our white wraps, we've become virgins paying homage to the sexual energies that are the source of life.

Finally we enter the corral and stand at our places around the circumference. We drop our shrouds. The drummers sing the soulful moonrise song. The moon mothers give each one of us a white feather. The dog soldiers smudge us with the pungent comfort of sage smoke. Boom! Boom! Boom! The drummers start the rhythm. We all blow our high-pitched whistles as we dance up to the tree. Thirty-five hands reach out, and we touch the tree together. It's a huge pillar of cottonwood. The bark is removed, so its smooth white surface glows like pale skin in the twilight. Red, black, yellow and white stripes circle it at the midpoint. At the top, streamers in the same colors float in the breeze. It's a monolithic phallus uniting earth and sky. I feel it activating my sexual energy. I know that by the end of the dance, I will fall in love with its huge beauty. I keep my eyes on it as we dance back to our places. For the next four days, while I dance, I won't take my eyes off this tree.

It dawns on me that I am part of a grand pagan rite. Now I understand why I have always been fascinated with ancient ruins, stone circles and sacred sites. The power that this dance is generating resides in those places. I can understand why the conquering cultures wanted to crush the old religions. I'm deeply grateful for this experience.

Just before sunset, thunder growls. Lightning shatters the sky. The clouds dump rain on us. The drums continue. We dance in the downpour. Red mud splatters our pristine ceremonial clothes. We slosh. We splash through puddles. Our whistles sputter. When the

## CHAPTER 20

# IMPACT!

I lie awake shivering in the dark silence. I feel every pebble on the hard ground under my squishy sleeping bag. I try to remember why I wanted to do this. In fact, I paid money to do this. Am I crazy? That's like paying tuition to go to boot camp. I wonder if Joseph would give me a refund if I go home now? Somehow, I don't think so. I begin to seriously doubt my own sanity.

My head clears for a moment, and I hear weeping. I listen silently while the man beside me cries like a baby. I wonder if he can really be more miserable than I am. I want to say something to comfort him, but I remember my vow of silence. I decide that he's crying for all of us. His sobbing goes on for what seems like hours without a pause. Finally, the woman on the other side of him asks what's wrong. He breaks the silence and tells his story.

"My wife has breast cancer. She had a mastectomy and a bone marrow transplant, but the doctors aren't giving her much hope. There's nothing else they can do. We have a six-year-old daughter. Then my vision went blurry while I was driving. I went to an eye doctor. I've got some disease of the retina. I'm going blind. I've already lost my sight in one eye. I can't help my wife. I can't take care of my daughter. I can't make a living. I can't even drive. What am I going to do?"

As I eavesdrop, my misery fades. I give thanks for my health, my sight, my work, my life. I think about Phoebe and how much she had to be thankful for once she was cancer-free...and how she refused to see it. Without speaking, I pray for the man beside me. I don't know his name, but I know his heart. I pray for healing for him and his wife and his daughter. I visualize him surrounded by golden healing light. I pray that the energy I'm sending is some comfort to him. He stops crying and falls asleep. I'm still cold and wet, but now it doesn't bother me.

I get up and go to the bathroom just as the light of dawn rims the horizon with a hot pink glow. It's a breathtaking sight. When I get back to my place, the dog soldiers begin to rustle around and prepare the camp. They smudge us. The drums greet the new day. We find the breath to make our whistles sing. We dance with the sun.

The sun blesses us by drying our damp clothes and soggy sleeping bags. We whistle and dance, dance and whistle. I feel at ease with the hunger and thirst. Finding the breath to whistle is difficult, but the drums lift me up, and my dance becomes effortless. When I walk to the bathroom, I find the husks of two cicadas stuck together as though they went on to their new forms while mating. In this magical natural world, even bugs embody love and transformation.

I'm in such deep silence that I'm not feeling much emotion or having many thoughts. Between dances, I just rest in stillness and enjoy the sensuality of the wind, the earthy fragrances, subtle sounds and silence. I think this must be what you feel just before death. It's very pleasant…almost euphoric.

Right now, I'm really enjoying watching the breeze blow the white sheet that I hung up as a sunshade. The rhythmic flow and unpredictable twists of the fabric are more fascinating than any movie I've ever seen.

Of course, my throat is painfully dry from blowing on my turkey bone whistle. I'm fantasizing about cranberry juice and grilled trout. Today, the moon mothers came around four times with wet hot towels for us. That's a luxury we never had during Drum Dance. The moisture absorbs through my skin. They also gave us a piece of fresh mint. I rub it on my face and put it in my mouth. It's wonderfully refreshing.

Several people hit the tree. Some run up and collide with it. Others sort of slide down it and collapse in tears. Then the moon mothers and dog soldiers run in and carry them out in a white sheet. Most of those people dance again after a rest. At one point, I feel the tree call me. For me, it's a sexual energy. The big phallus is seducing me, but I want the lovemaking to last as long as possible. I decide I won't hit the tree until it becomes irresistible.

After the last dance of the night, the moon mothers come around with medicine tea. It's actual liquid...only a couple of tablespoons but what a luxury! It almost feels like cheating. The weather is beautiful. It looks like no rain tonight.

I fall asleep easily and dream that I'm getting married. A Native American medicine man will perform the ceremony. My friends have gathered for the occasion. I'm not dressed in virgin white. Instead, I'm in a flowing gown of vivid turquoise, the color I'm wearing for the Sun Moon Dance. The wedding is about to begin, and I realize that something is missing. There's no groom. I turn to the medicine man, who's dressed in his finest feathers and jewelry. His face is painted with the colors of the medicine wheel.

"Who am I marrying?"

"You're marrying yourself."

In the dreamtime, this makes perfect sense. I proudly step up to the front of the crowd. The medicine man smudges me, shakes his rattle around me and sings a sacred song. He blesses a stunning necklace with multiple strands of raw turquoise nuggets and places it around my neck. I beam. He pronounces me married to myself. My friends applaud me.

I wake up. It's the dead of night. I put on my glasses to look at the stars. As soon as I scan the sky, I see a shooting star. I wish for an eternally healthy body. Immediately, another star blazes across the darkness. I wish for healthy, positive love.

The dog soldiers rouse us before dawn. We dance for about an hour, then put on our sheets and file out of the corral. We face east and greet the sunrise with the mesmerizing melodic song. We file back in the corral and continue the dance. I feel weak, and I'm less steady on my feet, but I'm euphoric. I have the sensation that I'm floating up to the pole and back. I ride the drumbeats like the current of a flowing river. There's a dull ache in my low back. I wonder if it's my kidneys beginning to fail from dehydration.

It takes a lot of energy to blow the turkey bone whistle. I think I've been saved when mine splits and stops working, but the dog soldiers bring me a new one. It's perfectly straight and brilliant white. I just breathe, and it lets out a shrill screech.

There's a big difference between three days without water and four days without water. Another twenty-four hours is a very long time when your body has already been pushed to the edge of survival. At the end of Drum Dance, I was in extreme discomfort, and my energy was alarmingly low. I'm at the same point now, and I won't be getting any water until tomorrow. I feel like I'm putting myself at serious risk. As I rest between dances, I find myself thinking how nice it would be to die this way. I'm not afraid. Dying seems like the path of least resistance. I don't have the energy to fight for life.

Disconnected surreal images flash through my head. I see horses, a dog, a buffalo painted with spiritual markings. I have a fragment of a dream about a dancer with a dog's face being carried out of the corral. He has something black...like a ball...in his mouth. I dream another fragment of a dog with red strings tied all over him. I have a vision of a bumblebee who tells me not to hang on to things, "Give them away!" I see a wolf and a pig hiding behind a bush.

The moon mothers bring us more mint. I suck the water off the leaves, chew some and rub the rest on my chakras. They bring us another wet towel. It feels divine. I rub myself down, then put the towel over my face. I have visions of a Sumo baby being carried in a chair and a young man capturing quail by sneaking up and grabbing them from behind.

I'm dreaming when the moon mothers wake me up and hand me a cup of WATER!!! I can't believe it. They say, "It's a medicine gift from your chief." It's so wonderfully WET! I sip gratitude. All the dancers get the same gift. Then we're blessed with more wet towels and mint.

I'm coming back to life. I'm so simple right now. My life is so good. I'm lucky. I'm grateful for my marriage and all it taught me about sex. I'm grateful for all my friends. I'm grateful for my years in the movie business. I'm grateful for my travels...to Thailand, Bali, Java, Hong Kong, Greece, Egypt, Japan, Mexico. I'm grateful for my lovers in their beautiful diversity...Mexican, African, East Indian, Scandinavian. I'm grateful for the ceremonies I've experienced...Zen meditation, Balinese blessings,

Taoist temples, the Drum Dance and now this Sun Moon Dance. I've had an amazing life so far. If I die now, it's OK. I have no unfinished business. If I live another fifty years, I'll be a kick-ass old lady with incredible stories to tell. The world is magical. I'm thrilled to be alive in it...and right now, I'm barely alive in it.

As I dance, I watch other dancers hit the tree. I commune with the tree as I push myself toward it and float back away from it. I shed tears of compassion for the suffering and struggle of humans on this earth. As I dance, I begin to realize that if I hit the tree, I can create a shift of energy and perception. As I dance, I come to understand that the shift affects not only the dancer but all of her ancestors and all of the humans who'll follow her on this earth.

So I must hit the tree with full commitment. Not for myself. What happens to me is not important. I must hit the tree for the children, for those who have gone before and those who will soon go on to the spirit world. I must hit the tree for the wounded ones, for the sick ones, for the men who treated me badly and for the woman who never liked me in the first place. I must hit the tree so they can all be shifted toward love.

Now I'm ready. I put on a pure white dress. The drums are quiet.

Joseph is moving around the corral checking with each dancer. When he comes to me, I tell him I'm ready to hit the tree. Everything has come into clear focus exactly as he said it would.

I say, "Start the drums!"

"In a few minutes."

I wait in euphoric stillness.

Boom! Boom! Boom! The drums start their heartbeat.

I dance up to the tree and back one time. I call out "Aho!" and run directly at the tree. I throw my head back so I'll hit the tree with my heart chakra.

Bam! The tree stops me in my tracks. I fall straight back with one leg on either side of the tree. I see stars, but I'm still conscious. I'm still alive!

The moon mothers rush in and fan me with turkey feather fans. The dog soldiers roll me onto a white sheet and carry me back to my place. They turn me around on my sleeping bag with my head toward the pole so I can start thinking with my heart. I'm crying. The moon mothers take off my shoes and fan me. They tell me the pain is gone. They don't understand that I'm not crying in pain. I'm not crying for any reason, but as I cry, anger rushes out of me and joy rushes in. They tell me to feel the hand of mother earth supporting me. I start laughing because I'm still alive. What a drama queen I've been! Chi begins buzzing in my hands, so I touch each of my chakras. Just as I finish doing that, the drums stop.

Joseph calls the dancers in to the pole. I don't go because I'm too weak to stand up. I hear him say, "This dance is over." He asks the dancers who can still walk to file out of the corral. As our chief, he has chosen to end the dance early because he can see that our spiritual goals have been accomplished. He explains that the dance actually has no end or no beginning. Since everything is made of vibrations, everything is eternally dancing...including humans.

One of the moon mothers helps me up rather brusquely and walks me out of the corral to the women's tipi. I sit on the ground. The ritual blessing and final feast will be tomorrow, but the dog soldiers give us water and fruit to sustain us through the night. I eat watermelon, orange slices, cantaloupe. It's delicious beyond description. I even sip a heavenly glass of lemonade. My mouth and throat are in ecstasy. I'm so grateful for this liquid, for this nourishment, for this amazing experience. I'm still crying. I feel a profound love for myself.

Tonight we get to sleep in our tents. We're supposed to move all of our things out of the corral. It seems like a lot of work, and I'm not up to it. One of the dog soldiers helps me. I eat yogurt, half a bran muffin and some cranberry juice. That's all I can handle, but I can feel my body recovering quickly. I'm amazed at how fast I'm coming back from near death.

I dream that I have a wound on my neck and another one on my finger. I wonder if I need stitches. The men I work with tell me it will be all right.

I get up about 4:30 to go to the bathroom. The tipi is silhouetted against the Milky Way. I stand and stare in awe. I've never seen a more magnificent sight.

# CHAPTER 21

# FEAR AND LOVE

The drums call us to the corral before dawn. We dance a couple of rounds. Then we go out and greet the sun with the sunrise song. We go back in and dance again. Joseph calls each dancer into the center of the corral to kneel for the water blessing. I'm the last one blessed. Shocking cold water splashes on the back of my neck. We go back to our places for silent meditation.

After about half an hour, Joseph steps into the center of the corral and speaks to us.

"This was my last Sun Moon Dance. As of today, I am retired." I gasp in shock. Other dancers cry out in protest. Joseph continues.

"Last fall, the doctors told me I had pancreatic cancer. I went to work on healing myself. By spring, they said it was gone, but I started to think about what would happen if I died. I realized I needed to empower other people to carry on my work." Many dancers are openly weeping. I'm one of them. Joseph keeps talking.

"It's time for you to take over and pass the ceremonies along to others. I'm leaving here and going back to the reservation. I want to spend more time with my family. I need to rest and continue to heal myself. I want to write and study with my elders. Now it's up to you to teach."

I can't teach. I'll be lost without his guidance. I'm just a beginner. I don't know anything. None of us knows anything compared to Joseph. I wonder if he's dying.

He dismisses us. It's time to go feast, but bewildered dancers mill around the corral. Some are in a daze. Some are still weeping. Some murmur to others in concern and amazement. I find Benito and ask him about the state of Joseph's health. He says Joseph is taking medication that's helping, and he's working with other shamanic healers who have given him a good prognosis. Benito feels Joseph's illness was caused by exhaustion, overwork and stress. Retirement is the key to his recovery.

My grief melts into respect. I see how selfless Joseph is. I'm in awe of his detachment and lack of ego. He was always clear that this work was not about power or fame or being worshipped. Now he walks his talk. He lets go of everything he created. He just hands it over to his students and walks away. I love this man. He's so humble and simple and deep.

I sit across from Joseph at the feast. I eat watermelon, grapes and vegetable soup. He tells me that the dance was over when he went around to check with all the dancers, but he extended it one round so I could hit the tree. He talks about the importance of the path of effort. To achieve supernatural power, you must choose to do things the most difficult way. Once you've achieved it, Spirit takes care of you, and things become effortless.

"Follow your visions…and then hang on for the ride."

I tell him about the euphoria and stillness I felt during the dance. He nods and smiles.

"Yes. That's what happens when you come into line with life."

I tell him about my dream of being wounded and some of the other strange images I saw.

"Once you dream it, it's done. You don't even need to ask anyone about it."

I stop asking him questions. My energy isn't completely back yet, so I take my time packing my gear. I drive to Albuquerque like a woman with a mission. I'm on a single-minded quest for two things: a mango yogurt smoothie and a hot shower...in that order. I find them both...and thoroughly enjoy the sensuous experience of cool sweetness and warm water.

Now I'm bathed, drinking iced tea and resting on clean sheets. I know these things with every cell: my heart is whole and complete, and Beautiful Painted Arrow will always be with me in timelessness. Now I fully understand the meaning of a phrase I heard him repeat many times, "You are the lover and the beloved." One question gnaws at me. How can Joseph be sick? He's a healer. He's grateful for his life. Why would he get cancer? I wanted to ask that question at the feast, but I didn't. I guess I didn't want to put him on the spot in front of so many people, or maybe I didn't want to look like I doubted him. I decide I'll stop by his place in the morning and ask him privately. I take myself out to dinner at my favorite restaurant, The Range Cafe in Bernalillo. I eat a perfectly grilled boneless trout and salad with raspberry vinaigrette. It tastes like heaven on earth. I thank Spirit for the nourishment. I sit at a table with some of the other dancers, but there's very little conversation. We're all still in silence.

In the morning, Joseph's working in his garden when I pull into his driveway. We hug. He gives me seeds from his hollyhocks to plant in my garden in Los Angeles.

"Joseph, with everything you know about healing, I don't understand how you could get cancer."

"There are many levels of knowledge about healing, you know. There's always more for us to learn. The only way to learn it is by healing ourselves."

"And you agreed to it before you came here."

He smiled, "You're a good student."

"I am the lover, and I am the beloved. I really got what that means at the dance."

"There are many levels of loving too. You can't move to a deeper one unless you get involved with somebody."

"My marriage was a mistake I don't want to make again."

"You're like the alcoholic who's stopped drinking and gone to AA. As long as he doesn't take a drink, he's got his life under control. But he's still an alcoholic. He hasn't addressed the real reason behind his addiction...which is his fear that he's not love-able. Marsha, you've done the work. You've confronted the fear."

"So if I get involved with a man, I won't be addicted to him?"

"I don't know, but I think you should test yourself. You're a different person now. You'll handle a relationship in a whole different way."

"There's still so much I need to learn. How can you say I'm empowered to teach? I don't feel qualified."

"Just remember, it all boils down to one lesson. Before you make a decision or take an action, ask yourself this: Is what I'm about to do going to create fear and separation...or love? If the answer is fear and separation, don't do it. Never ever take an action or make a decision from a place of fear. It's better not to do anything at all than to act out of fear."

"That's so simple."

"It assumes you know the difference between fear and intuition...and I think you do."

"I feel so lucky to have been able to work with you."

"I feel lucky to have worked with you too. You're a beautiful person. Don't ever forget it."

I turn and walk to my car. At the door, I turn back and say, "You're so amazing." He makes a gesture like he's brushing it off.

I cry for the first few miles as I drive north toward Santa Fe. My eyes drink in the New Mexico landscape. My heart fills with love for the land, the clouds, the sage and cedar. I park close to the Plaza. I buy the world's most delicious frozen lemonade and drink it standing in line for the Georgia O'Keefe museum. As always, her work is mystical, soulful, inspiring. There are some paintings I've never seen before: a human skull with a broken pot, antelope antlers against a peachy desert landscape, a ghostly full moon peeking through a hole in a pelvis.

As I walk back to my car, an old Hispanic man stops me. A well-worn cowboy hat shades his weathered face. He comments on how hot the weather is. I agree. He asks me if I'm from Santa Fe. I say I'm not.

"Do you go to church?"

"I go to many churches."

" People say The Lord's Prayer, but they don't love."

"That's true."

"But you love people."

"Yes. I do."

"The only way there will be peace in the world is if we love each other."

"That's true."

He puts his hands on my cheeks, kisses me and says,

"I can tell you're a friendly person."

He kisses me again.

He repeats, "The only way there will be peace in the world is if we love each other."

He kisses me a third time. I bid him "goodbye" and walk to my car. Was he just a crazy old man who'd been out in the sun too long? Did I imagine him? Was he a magical manifestation of Spirit? Whatever he was, I feel like Spirit was letting me know that my love shines out to strangers, that I've learned my lessons, that I'm working for peace with every breath of my life.

As soon as I arrive at Marsha Mason's ranch, she offers margaritas made with all natural margarita mix from the Wild Oats market in Santa Fe. My body is far too sensitive to deal with alcohol, so I have mine sans tequila. I ask her what's going on with my screenplay. She says she thinks we should have a reading. She'll get her actor friends to read the roles so we can hear how it sounds. It seems like a good idea to me. I ask what kind of response it got from her agent. She hesitates before she answers.

"He's not convinced it has commercial potential."

In Hollywood, that's the kiss of death. She adds that she still believes in the project, but her words don't ring true. I ask myself if she's acting out of fear or out of love. The answer is fear. She's afraid her career is fading. She found a project that spoke to her, but now she's afraid it's a box office loser. I feel like she wants out. The reading will provide a reason to say it's not working.

Part of me wants to say, "Your agent's wrong. It will be successful. We have to fight for what we believe in! Every studio passed on *Star Wars*." Or "I'll rewrite it. The Mafia can be chasing her. I'll add a few explosions." But I ask myself, "If you say either of those things, will you be speaking out of love or out of fear?" The answer is fear. I'm afraid to lose this deal. I'm afraid I'll never make it as a writer. I'm afraid my mother's spirit will never accomplish her task.

I don't say anything. I sip my virgin margarita and watch the thunderheads stack up over the vast void of the desert. When I consider everything that happened with Phoebe and all I've learned from Joseph, the screenplay seems unimportant. I silently scold myself for asking for help with such a trivial task, but I know I've accomplished something greater than that. Now I'm passionately living a vivid life. Trying to sell the screenplay was just the bait that led me down this sacred path. It's walking the path that's important, not reaching the goal. Marsha tells me she's thinking about starting a medicinal herb farm. The unspoken subtext is that her heart is no longer in Hollywood. She's taking the first steps on a new path herself.

I call Ray. He takes me out to dinner at Café Pascal, my favorite restaurant in Santa Fe. It's an old diner turned trendy. It's crowded with folk art, beautiful people and bright red gladiolas. I eat a burrito stuffed with grilled salmon, goat cheese and black beans. It's divine. I try to explain the Sun Moon Dance to Ray. He doesn't get it. I don't think he gets me. I see fear in his eyes. He doesn't want to be alone. He thinks I can take that fear away. I know better now.

In the morning, Sam calls from Columbus. He's playful and funny and restless. I tell him about Joseph's retirement. He's impressed that my guru would voluntarily give up the reins of power. Sam says he wants to see me. I say I want to see him. He asks if he can come to Los Angeles and stay with me. I feel the fear rush in.

"How long do you want to stay?"

"Maybe a month."

Before I answer, I ask myself if I'm making this decision out of fear or out of love. The choice becomes clear. Refusing is an act of fear. Agreeing is opening up to love.

"Yes. Please come."

"I'll be there in a couple of weeks."

On the way to Albuquerque airport, I pass the turnoff to Phoebe's house. I think about the garden I planted and wonder how it looks now. I wonder if Phoebe has grown or withered and died. I wonder if she ever wonders about me.

As my plane gets ready to take off, a thunderstorm rumbles in. We sit on the runway and watch lightning strike the airfield. We finally take off and pass a rainstorm off to our left. It's a gossamer veil backlit with sunlight. As we fly by, a rainbow pillar appears, then splits into a double arc. The two rainbows merge into a single column of illuminated colors. I feel like New Mexico is giving me a glorious farewell. We fly into a thick cloudbank as I leave the Land of Enchantment.

Back in Los Angeles, my bliss is shattered by severe pain in my low back. My chiropractor, a polite and proper woman from Japan, diagnoses the problem as whiplash. She asks if I've been in an accident recently.

"Well, I hit a tree."

"Were you driving?"

"No. I wasn't in a car."

"I don't understand."

"I ran into a tree...intentionally." She does her best to keep a straight face as I explain the Sun Moon Dance to her. I can tell she thinks I'm an absolute lunatic...but she helps me anyway. I call

Joseph and tell him about my whiplash. He laughs.

"I guess you agreed to it before you came here, but it's definitely a first in the history of the Sun Moon Dance."

"Or I'm the first to admit it."

I spend the next couple weeks working on healing myself so I'll be in shape to enjoy Sam. The dark sister and the blonde doctor rent a basement room in a whorehouse…

## CHAPTER 22

# CROSSING OVER

"Marsha? It's Lenore Johnson, Phoebe's sister."

She'd never called me before, so I knew she had bad news.

"Hi Lenore. What's going on?"

"Phoebe's dying."

"I'm sorry to hear that. Are you with her?"

"Yes. In Albuquerque. Do you want to see her?"

"Does she want to see me?"

"I didn't ask her. I thought you might want to come here."

"Yeah. I do."

I fly to Albuquerque and take a cab directly to St Joseph's hospital. Phoebe is sleeping when I enter her room. I haven't seen her for months. She's bald and her body is swollen from more chemotherapy. She looks like a baby. I marvel at the thinness of the veil between being born and dying. Lenore sits beside her bed. We exchange whispered greetings. Lenore says she needs a break and goes to the cafeteria. I take her seat.

After half an hour, Phoebe wakes up. She doesn't seem particularly surprised to see me. I ask her how she feels.

"Not good. It's hard to swallow. I feel like I'm choking on my saliva. Hand me that suction tube."

I hand her a clear plastic wand attached to a plastic tube. She vacuums out her mouth. I tell her I love her. She avoids looking me in the eye.

"If you think you can get me to say I love you, you're wrong."

"It doesn't matter. I still love you."

"You remember when you asked me if I was jealous of you?"

"Yeah. After Carlsbad."

"I said I wasn't. That was a lie. I was jealous but not about your boyfriend. I was jealous of your health."

"I know I'm lucky...and I'm grateful."

"So what happened with your boyfriend?"

"He came and stayed with me in L.A. for a couple of months. We had fun and a lot of good sex. Now he's going to language school in Monterey to get a Master's in Spanish."

"Did you break up?"

"Not really, but he'd like to have a family, so I assume he's looking for a younger woman."

"Asshole!"

"No. He's a good man. I'm really grateful for the time we spent together. The age difference means we have different needs. It doesn't mean we don't love each other."

"Bullshit! He's an asshole."

I stand, kiss her on the forehead, say "Goodbye" and walk to the door. Her voice stops me.

"Do you think you're better than me?"

I turn and look her in the eye.

"Phoebe, I don't have the power to heal you. It's important that you understand that. I think when I was trying to heal you, I lectured you about what you needed to do to get well. I'm sure that was really obnoxious. I'm sure I lectured Jack the same way the whole time we were married. That's about my own insecurity. I feel more powerful when I'm telling other people how to straighten out their lives. Now I know I'm not perfect...and that's

OK with me. I also know that other people aren't perfect...and that's OK with me too. In lots of ways, my life is a mess. My movie deal fell apart. My lover is looking for a younger woman. The assistant director work has all gone to Canada, and I'm going broke fast. I do all this healing work with Joseph because I'm in a lot of pain myself. Isn't it obvious that I'm doing a lot of things wrong in my life? I don't want to admit it because I don't want to start criticizing myself. If I criticize myself, then I'll criticize you."

The room is silent. Phoebe chokes when she starts to speak. She reaches for the suction tube and vacuums out her mouth. Finally, she puts down the tube.

"You said so much." She starts to cry. "I know I judge myself. I've been really hard on myself."

"You were always alright with me."

"My therapist makes me look at stuff I don't like to see about myself...like how I project low self-esteem then get mad at people who offer advice."

"Yeah. You do that."

"Marsha..."

By now, she's sobbing. I recognize the rattle in her cough. She's choking on saliva and desperately grasping for the suction tube. I place it in her hand. I pull tissues out of the box and tuck them into her other hand. I sit down in the chair. She's crying too hard to vacuum her mouth. I take the tube and do it for her. As I touch her lips, I remember spooning persimmon into my mother's mouth. Tears stream down my cheeks. Phoebe wipes away tears of her own.

"...thanks for saying what you said. And thanks for that meditation about the crystal sword. That really helped."

"Phoebe, are you afraid to die?"

"Yes."

"We all die, you know. It's OK. It doesn't mean you fucked up."
As I say that, my words shatter something brittle in her. I feel a
sudden release and see the murky energy of constricted anger flow
out of her. I continue in a whisper. "I've been there. I danced right up to the threshold. It's quiet
there. Simple. Peaceful."
She sinks back into her pillows. Her face relaxes. Her lips turn
up into a slight smile. She closes her eyes. She looks serene and
beautiful like an elegant stone Buddha. I reach for her hand. My
fingers touch her little finger...polarity. I realize Phoebe got stuck
in polarity. Love was all around her. She never moved into unity
with it.

"Phoebe...it's all right now. In fact, it's a gas."

Phoebe never regains consciousness. She dies a couple of hours
later. Her face still radiates peace. Lenore and I are by her side. We
hold hands, weep and watch the sunset through the hospital
window. The sky streaks with luminous pink and gold. Then all
light fades into darkness.

I call Joseph. I ask him about his health. He tells me his
pancreatic cancer hasn't recurred. He's cured himself completely.
He gives me instructions for helping Phoebe make her transition to
the spirit world. That night, Lenore and I sleep soundly.

In the morning, I go out to track down everything I'll need for
Phoebe's final blessing. In a shop near the university, I find a small
deerskin pouch. At the supermarket, I pick up a large candle in
glass and small amounts of Phoebe's favorite foods. I go home. I
make a peanut butter and jelly sandwich on whole wheat bread. I

put a sliver of it in the pouch along with a couple of fresh raspberries, a morsel of cheesecake, a Dorito and a Hall's Mentholyptus cough drop. I call the mortuary and ask for an appointment to see Phoebe's body "for religious reasons." They give me one that afternoon.

At the scheduled time, I show up at the mortuary with the pouch, a feather fan, some white sage and an abalone shell. A polite Asian man in a dark suit greets me and asks me to wait a few minutes while they move Phoebe into "a slumber room" for viewing. Ten minutes later, he ushers me into a small, dark, windowless room. The only thing in the room is a long narrow cardboard box. He takes the lid off the box. Inside is some stiff, long, lumpy object completely wrapped in a white sheet. I presume this is Phoebe's body. She's shrouded like a dancer at the Sun Moon Dance. The mortician says, "I'll give you some privacy" and leaves the room. He closes the door behind him. I'm shut in a small dark room alone with a dead body. I whisper, "Great Spirit, give me the courage to help Phoebe cross over." I light the sage in the abalone shell. I fan the smoke over myself, then over Phoebe's body. I pass the pouch through the smoke and slip it inside the shroud. I place it over her heart. I say, "Great Spirit, bless, guide and protect Phoebe as she makes this transition...for all my relations." I put out the sage and escape into the sunlight.

On the day Phoebe is cremated, I light the candle. I let it burn for four days. At the end of the fourth day, I blow out the flame and immediately take a cold shower. As I shiver in the frigid spray, I pray out loud, "Phoebe, thank you for being my teacher. Your journey inspired me to heal myself. You taught me that trying to rescue people I love only disempowers them. I'm deeply grateful for the sacrifice you made so I could learn and grow. I honor your life and death…and while you're in the spirit world, please help me find my way in this one."

For all my relations.

Now I see hummingbirds everywhere.

# EPILOGUE

During the Sun Moon Dance, Joseph asked us what it means to "live life in rhythm". He said, "The drum is not the drum. The earth is not the earth. The trees are not the trees. The fire is not the fire. Your legs are not your legs. Think about what these things really are. This is not an intellectual exercise."

I sat by the fire and stared into it. I saw that the drum is cycles of silence and vibration. Living life in rhythm is letting the cycles of life move you without wasting energy by trying to control them. To live life in rhythm is to be energized by the alternating opposites of happy/sad, work/play, feast/famine, solitude/relationship, birth/death.

The fire is simply energy, the heat of the life force, the transformer. As I stared into the fire, a phrase popped into my mind: "This is all there is. There is nothing else to know."

# HOW TO DANCE YOUR DANCE

Beautiful Painted Arrow retired from leading ceremonies in 1997, but dancers dance on all over the world under the leadership of his students. If the idea of participating in a dance fast resonates with you, you will find an opportunity. Understand that these are not Native American dances. They are open to all people who seek inspiration to live a life of high potential. The dances do not promote any specific religion or creed.

In the early 1980s, Beautiful Painted Arrow had a vision that he was to promote the building of Peace Chambers throughout the world. These oval-shaped structures (somewhat similar to kivas) are designated for chanting certain sacred sounds which create the vibrations most conducive to world peace. Today there are over 70 peace chambers throughout the world including the United States, Europe, United Kingdom, Canada, South America, Australia, South Africa and Israel. The sacred dances are often hosted by Peace Chamber keepers. Visit www.peacechamber.com for a list of Peace Chambers throughout the world. Some Peace Chambers have their dance schedule posted on their websites. Visit:

www.birdsongpeacechamber.com,

www.centerforpeace.us,

www.earthsongpeacechamber.com,

www.watersongpeacechamber.com.

Besides the Drum Dance and the Sun Moon Dance, there are other dances, originally envisioned by Beautiful Painted Arrow or his students, which invoke certain spiritual energies. The Long Dance is an all night dance that works with subconscious. There are some dances just for men and some just for women. You will instinctively know which dance is right for you. Once you commit to a specific dance, the coordinator will send you instructions about how to prepare for the dance, what to bring, what to wear, when to arrive and other details. Peace Chambers may offer other spiritual opportunities including sweatlodges, fire ceremonies and chanting for world peace.

You can learn more about Beautiful Painted Arrow, his visions and his teachings by reading his books (available on Amazon.com and bookstores):

*Beautiful Painted Arrow: Stories and Teachings from the Native American Tradition*, Joseph E. Rael, Element Books (April 1992)

*Being and Vibration*, Joseph Rael, Mary Elizabeth Marlow, Council Oak Books (September 2002)

*The Way of Inspiration: Wah-Mah-Chi*, Joseph Rael, Council Oak Books; 1st edition (November 1996)

*Ceremonies of the Living Spirit*, Joseph Rael, Council Oak Books; 1st ed edition (February 1998)

*House of Shattering Light: Life As an American Indian Mystic*, Joseph Rael, Publisher: Council Oak Books (April 2003)

Beautiful Painted Arrow's inspirational lectures have been captured on five DVDs: *Footprints of a Soul, Inspirations of the Metaphoric Mind, Passageway to the Infinite Self, Sound Beings* and *Ceremonies of Awakening* (which deals specifically with the dances and sweatlodge) available at:

http://www.martialartslive.com/.

Other teachers and visionaries also have much to offer. Brooke Medicine Eagle shares related insights in her books:

*Buffalo Woman Comes Singing*, Brooke Medicine Eagle,

Ballantine Books; 1st edition (December 1991)

*The Last Ghost Dance : A Guide for Earth Mages*, Brooke Medicine Eagle, Wellspring/Ballantine (October 2000)

*The Last Ghost Dance* includes a chapter devoted to the history and future of group trance dances. She travels extensively and teaches workshops at her center in Montana. Visit www.medicineeagle.com for her schedule, or call her at 406 883-4686.

The history and technique of drum journeying is explored in detail in Michael Harner's classic book:

*The Way of the Shaman*, Michael Harner, HarperSanFrancisco; 10th Anniversary edition (October 1990)

Classes and workshops in basic and advanced shamanic techniques are offered through his organization: Foundation for Shamanic Studies, 415 380-8282, www.shamanicstudies.org

The basic world view and philosophy of personal responsibility central to shamanic healing is beautifully explained in the work of Don Miguel Ruiz, particularly his books:

*The Four Agreements*, Don Miguel Ruiz, Amber-Allen Publishing (November 1997)

*The Mastery of Love: A Practical Guide to the Art of Relationship: A Toltec Wisdom Book*, Don Miguel Ruiz, Amber-Allen Publishing (May 1999)

Along with his son Don Jose Ruiz, Don Miguel offers workshops, lectures and spiritual journeys to Teotihuacan, Mexico. Visit www.miguelruiz.com for more information.

As you explore this world of shamanism and spirit dancing, listen with your heart. Trust your intuition and your dance will dance you. Aho!

# ABOUT THE AUTHOR

While studying journalism at the University of Southern California, Marsha Scarbrough was named Guest Feature Editor of *Mademoiselle Magazine*, an honor that included travel to New York City and Peru.

As a graduate of the Directors Guild of America's prestigious Assistant Directors Training Program, Marsha spent 17 years scheduling, planning and running the sets of major feature films, prime time television series, movies of the week and network sitcoms. She has handled logistics, organization and administration for various directors including Clint Eastwood, Leonard Nimoy, Blake Edwards and Carl Reiner.

Marsha wrote, produced and directed the award-winning children's video, *The Magic of Martial Arts*, which has been honored with the Gold Award from the National Association of Parenting Publications, the Award of Excellence from Film Advisory Board and the KIDS FIRST! endorsement from the Coalition for Quality Children's Media.

As a freelance journalist, Marsha has had over 75 articles published in national magazines such as *TV Guide, Body & Soul, Natural Home & Garden* and *Millimeter: The Motion Picture and Television Production Magazine*. As a contributing editor for *Written By: The Magazine of the Writers Guild of America, west*, Marsha interviews Hollywood's most prominent screen and television writers.

Along the way, Marsha traveled with Buddhist teacher Joan Halifax, danced with movement guru Gabrielle Roth, earned a brown belt in karate from martial arts legend Tak Kubota, participated in healing ceremonies with Native American mystic Beautiful Painted Arrow/Joseph Rael and produced workshops for Nigerian master drummer/Yoruba ceremonial leader Ayo Adeyemi.

For more information, visit her website at www.marshascarbrough.com. To contact Marsha about teaching a workshop or speaking at an event, email her at mscarb1234@aol.com.

# O

is a symbol of the world,
of oneness and unity. O Books
explores the many paths of wholeness
and spiritual understanding which
different traditions have developed down
the ages. It aims to bring this knowledge
in accessible form, to a general readership,
providing practical spirituality to today's seekers.

For the full list of over 200 titles covering:

- CHILDREN'S PRAYER, NOVELTY AND GIFT BOOKS
- CHILDREN'S CHRISTIAN AND SPIRITUALITY
- CHRISTMAS AND EASTER
- RELIGION/PHILOSOPHY
- SCHOOL TITLES
- ANGELS/CHANNELLING
- HEALING/MEDITATION
- SELF-HELP/RELATIONSHIPS
- ASTROLOGY/NUMEROLOGY
- SPIRITUAL ENQUIRY
- CHRISTIANITY, EVANGELICAL
  AND LIBERAL/RADICAL
- CURRENT AFFAIRS
- HISTORY/BIOGRAPHY
- INSPIRATIONAL/DEVOTIONAL
- WORLD RELIGIONS/INTERFAITH
- BIOGRAPHY AND FICTION
- BIBLE AND REFERENCE
- SCIENCE/PSYCHOLOGY

Please visit our website,
**www.O-books.net**

## Daughters of the Earth

Cheryl Straffon

*In her new book Cheryl combines legend, landscape and women's ceremonies to create a wonderful mixture of Goddess experience in the present day. Her knowledge ranges from the paleolithic and neolithic eras to modern times as we follow her explorations of sacred sites from the Cave of the Bear in Crete to the Cave of Cats at Rathcroghan in Ireland. A feast of information, ideas, facts and visions.* **Kathy Jones**, co-founder of the Glastonbury Goddess Conference and author of The Ancient British Goddess

1846940168 240pp **£11.99 $21.95**

## The Goddess, the Grail and the Lodge

**The Da Vinci code and the real origins of religion**

Alan Butler

5th printing

*This book rings through with the integrity of sharing time-honoured revelations. As a historical detective, following a golden thread from the great Megalithic cultures, Alan Butler vividly presents a compelling picture of the fight for life of a great secret and one that we simply can't afford to ignore.* From the foreword by **Lynn Picknett** & **Clive Prince**

1903816696 360pp 230/152mm **£12.99 $19.95**

## The Gods Within

**An interactive guide to archetypal therapy**

Peter Lemesurier

*Whether you enjoy analyzing your family and friends or looking for ways*

*to explain or excuse your own strengths and weaknesses, this book provides a whole new slant. It can be read just for fun, but there is an uncanny ring of truth to it. Peter Lemesurier combines scholarship with wry humour, a compulsive mixture.* **Anna Corser**, Physiotherapy Manager
1905047991 260pp 30 b/w photos **£14.99 $24.95**

## Maiden, Mother, Crone
### Voices of the Goddess
Claire Hamilton

Written in the first person, these provocative and surprising renderings of Celtic tales take us on a challenging journey in which the twelve most ancient and extraordinary goddesses of the land reveal their light and dark faces. In bringing their symbolism to life for today they restore our earlier understanding of war, sex and death.
1905047398 240pp **£12.99 $24.95**

## The Sacred Wheel of the Year
Tess Ward

A book of prayers intended for individual use. Divided into monthly sections, with a week or prayers for each, it incorporates Celtic Christian and Celtic Pagan traditions in a single pattern of prayer.
1905047959 260pp **£11.99 $21.95**